Pillsbury

MAKE MINE
CHOCOLATE

Ottenheimer Publishers, Inc.

Publisher: Ronald J. Kos
Managing Editor: Diane B. Anderson
Associate Editor: Elaine Christiansen
Subscription Coordinator: Vicki Kuhlmann
Publications Assistant: Karen Buettner
Food Editor and Food Stylist: Barb Standal
Contributing Editor: Heather Randall King
Home Economists: Pillsbury Consumer Center
Nutrition Coordinator: Patricia Godfrey, R.D.
Design, Production: Tad Ware & Company, Inc.
Photography: Studio 3

This edition published by arrangement
with Ottenheimer Publishers, Inc.,
distributed by Wholesale Warehousing Industries, Inc.,
250 Granton Drive, Richmond Hill, Ontario, Canada, L4B 1H7.

Cover Photo: Creamy Chocolate Lace Cheesecake p. 44

Contents

Make Mine Chocolate!

If your first choice is usually chocolate, you won't be surprised to learn that the literal translation for the cacao tree's botanical name, Theobroma cacao, is "food of the gods." Many varieties of the lush, evergreen cacao tree grow in tropical orchards near the equator. From the seeds, or beans, produced by these trees come all types of chocolate used for baking, eating and drinking. Although many refer to the seeds as "cocoa beans," "cacao" is technically correct and clears up the common misconception that the beans come from the coconut palm tree.

Workers, mainly in hot, humid regions of Africa and South America, harvest the pods or fruit by cutting them from branches and removing up to 50 tiny almond-shaped seeds from each. At this stage, the beans bear little resemblance to the product which will be refined by cleaning, fermenting, drying and removing husks. The "nibs," cacao seeds without shells, are rich in cocoa butter, the natural fat of the bean. Cocoa butter is released when the nibs are ground. Cocoa butter and ground cacao form a rich paste known as chocolate liquor. This product is the basis for all chocolate products.

According to historical records, chocolate lovers abounded before Columbus arrived in America. Aztec and Maya Indians sipped on a cold, bitter beverage made from the ground beans, and Aztecs used the precious commodity as a form of barter. Legends of the time reveal that these Indian people revered the beans as a gift from paradise which had been sown on earth by a prophet to offer universal wisdom to those who ate of them.

Chocolate's international fame and popularity began in the 1500's when explorer Hernando Cortes carried cacao beans back to Spain. After some experimentation, Europeans found that

> *...Aztec Indian people revered the cocoa beans as a gift from paradise...*

warming and sweetening the brew enhanced the innate flavor. Thus transformed, it quickly became a very fashionable drink in royal courts across the Continent.

Despite chocolate's enthusiastic reception, it wasn't until the 19th century that methods were perfected for producing chocolate for eating. Variations in processing techniques, amounts of cocoa butter and the addition of ingredients like sweeteners and flavorings determine the types and quality levels of chocolate. The coarse-grained product of early experimentation has been replaced by today's creamy confections. The largest consumer of chocolate in the world? You guessed it. The United States!

Tips for Cooking with Chocolate

♥ *Facilitate melting* by breaking chocolate blocks, bars or chunks into smaller, uniform pieces.

♥ Place chocolate pieces for melting in pan or dish that is *completely dry* and use *thoroughly dry utensils* for stirring.

♥ For *range top melting*, place chocolate pieces in *heavy* saucepan. Avoid scorching and stiffening by *stirring constantly* over *low, even heat* not exceeding a temperature of 110°. Melted chocolate should feel *lukewarm, not hot*, to the touch.

♥ If chocolate should harden or stiffen during stove-top melting, *add 1 teaspoon shortening or oil* (not butter) for each ounce of chocolate and stir until texture returns to normal.

♥ For *microwave oven melting*, place chocolate pieces in microwave-safe container. A 1-ounce square will take 1 to 2 minutes on MEDIUM setting to become soft enough to stir to smooth consistency. Add 10 seconds per each additional ounce. Six ounces *chocolate chips* need 2½ to 3½ minutes of MEDIUM microwave heat to become soft enough to stir. Add 2 to 3 minutes for each additional cup of chips. NOTE: Most chocolates melted by microwave method will retain original shape even though they have softened to proper consistency. Look for *glossy appearance* and *stir* before adding additional time.

♥ Recipes in this cookbook were tested in 650-watt microwave ovens. Because microwave ovens vary by manufacturer, it may be necessary to adjust the cooking times.

EACH RECIPE IN THIS BOOK GIVES COMPLETE INSTRUCTIONS FOR PROPER HANDLING AND HEATING OF THE TYPE OF CHOCOLATE FEATURED. We urge you to follow these suggestions carefully to avoid scorching, stiffening and other problems which can occur when cooking with chocolate.

Chocolate Choices in This Cookbook

UNSWEETENED CHOCOLATE
The basic chocolate from which all other products are made. It is molded into 1-oz. blocks and packed eight to a carton.

SEMI-SWEET CHOCOLATE
Unsweetened chocolate with sugar, additional cocoa butter and flavorings added. It is also molded into 1-oz. blocks and packed eight to a carton or formed into chocolate chips and sold in 6 or 12-oz. packages.

SWEET COOKING CHOCOLATE
(German sweet chocolate) — similar to semi-sweet chocolate, but with a higher proportion of sugar and packaged in 4-oz. bars.

MILK CHOCOLATE
Sweet chocolate with milk added and packaged in various-size bars and shapes.

WHITE CHOCOLATE
Not really chocolate in the true sense; a blend of milk and sugar cooked until it condenses into a solid. Some types contain cocoa butter; others contain artificial flavoring. Available in bars or chunks.

ALMOND BARK
(Vanilla-flavored candy coating) — a compound made with vegetable fats instead of cocoa butter, with coloring and flavorings added. Available in 1½-lb. packages or in blocks and round discs where candy making supplies are sold.

UNSWEETENED COCOA
Pure chocolate with most of the cocoa butter removed and ground into powder form, available in 8 or 16-oz. cans.

CHOCOLATE-FLAVORED SYRUP
A combination of cocoa, corn syrup and flavoring; available in various-size jars or cans.

Our Most Requested Chocolate Recipes

Chocolate Cherry Bars p. 7

Our Most Requested Chocolate Recipes

Because YOU asked for them!

Some recipes, from kitchens across America, survived stringent testing and rigorous competition to take honored positions as Bake-Off® winners. Others were carefully created by our own home economists. And still others were inspired by convenience products like Pillsbury cake and brownie mixes, Ready To Spread Frostings and All Ready Pie Crusts. Whatever the origin of our most requested recipes, one thing is evident—each and every one holds a revered place in personal recipe collections across the country.

We took cues from you when selecting the popular choices for this chapter. Each day consumers telephone and write for copies of lost or misplaced Pillsbury favorites. This confirms time and again the timelessness of such famous favorites as Oatmeal Carmelitas, Snappy Turtle Cookies, French Silk Chocolate Pie and Tunnel of Fudge Cake. Other sweets, which have appeared over the years on product packages or in our cookbooks, offer a tasty tale of how baking techniques and products have changed, with the same high quality and good flavor always reliable.

Because these recipes are so important to you and to us, we continually update ingredients and methods so you can count on original goodness, prepared 1980's style. Never have desserts so delicious been so easy!

Deliciously easy, this often requested Bake-Off® Contest grand prize winning recipe uses few ingredients.

Chocolate Cherry Bars

BARS

    1 pkg. Pillsbury Plus Devil's Food Cake Mix
21-oz. can cherry fruit pie filling
    1 teaspoon almond extract
    2 eggs, beaten

FROSTING

    1 cup sugar
    5 tablespoons margarine or butter
    ⅓ cup milk
6-oz. pkg. (1 cup) semi-sweet chocolate chips

Heat oven to 350°F. Grease and flour 15x10-inch jelly roll pan or 13x9-inch pan. In large bowl, combine all bar ingredients; stir until well mixed. Pour into prepared pan. Bake at 350°F. in jelly roll pan for 20 to 30 minutes or in 13x9-inch pan for 25 to 30 minutes or until toothpick inserted in center comes out clean.

In small saucepan, combine sugar, margarine and milk. Bring to a boil; boil 1 minute, stirring constantly. Remove from heat; stir in chocolate chips until smooth. Pour over warm bars. Cool. Cut into bars; garnish as desired. 36 bars.

HIGH ALTITUDE—Above 3500 Feet: Bake at 375°F. in 15x10-inch jelly roll pan for 20 to 30 minutes or in 13x9-inch pan for 25 to 30 minutes.

NUTRITION INFORMATION PER SERVING

SERVING SIZE: 1 BAR		PERCENT U.S. RDA PER SERVING	
CALORIES	150	PROTEIN	2%
PROTEIN	1g	VITAMIN A	2%
CARBOHYDRATE	26g	VITAMIN C	*
FAT	5g	THIAMINE	2%
CHOLESTEROL	15mg	RIBOFLAVIN	2%
SODIUM	140mg	NIACIN	*
POTASSIUM	60mg	CALCIUM	4%
		IRON	2%

*Contains less than 2% of the U.S. RDA of this nutrient.

Your family can participate in making this recipe by helping to unwrap the caramels. Favorite flavors and textures are incorporated in this popular bar.

Caramel Layer Choco-Squares

14-oz. pkg. vanilla caramels, unwrapped
    ⅓ cup evaporated milk
    1 pkg. Pillsbury Plus German Chocolate Cake Mix
    1 cup chopped nuts
    ½ cup margarine or butter, softened
    2 tablespoons evaporated milk
6-oz. pkg. (1 cup) semi-sweet chocolate chips

Heat oven to 350°F. In medium saucepan over low heat, combine caramels and ⅓ cup evaporated milk, stirring constantly until caramels are melted. In large bowl, combine cake mix, nuts, margarine and 2 tablespoons evaporated milk. Mix well. Press half of dough into bottom of ungreased 13x9-inch pan; reserve remaining dough for topping.

Bake at 350°F. for 8 minutes. Sprinkle chocolate chips evenly over partially baked crust. Carefully spread caramel mixture over chocolate chips. Crumble reserved dough over caramel mixture. Return to oven and bake 15 to 18 minutes or until filling is set. Cool completely; cut into squares. 36 bars.

HIGH ALTITUDE—Above 3500 Feet: No change.

NUTRITION INFORMATION PER SERVING

SERVING SIZE: 1 SQUARE		PERCENT U.S. RDA PER SERVING	
CALORIES	180	PROTEIN	2%
PROTEIN	2g	VITAMIN A	2%
CARBOHYDRATE	23g	VITAMIN C	*
FAT	9g	THIAMINE	4%
CHOLESTEROL	0mg	RIBOFLAVIN	4%
SODIUM	160mg	NIACIN	2%
POTASSIUM	80mg	CALCIUM	4%
		IRON	4%

*Contains less than 2% of the U.S. RDA of this nutrient.

French Silk Chocolate Pie p. 10

French Silk Chocolate Pie

CRUST
1 (15-oz.) pkg. Pillsbury All Ready Pie Crusts

FILLING
3 oz. (3 squares) unsweetened chocolate, cut up
¾ cup butter, softened
1 cup sugar
½ teaspoon vanilla
¾ cup frozen cholesterol-free egg product, thawed
½ cup sweetened whipped cream Chocolate Curls (see Index), if desired

Heat oven to 450°F. Prepare pie crust according to package directions for **unfilled one-crust pie** using 9-inch pie pan.* (Refrigerate remaining crust for a later use.) Bake at 450°F. for 9 to 11 minutes or until lightly browned. Cool.

Melt chocolate in small saucepan over low heat; cool. In small bowl, beat butter until fluffy; add sugar gradually, beating until light and fluffy. Blend in cooled chocolate and vanilla. Add egg product ¼ cup at a time, beating at high speed 2 minutes after each addition. Beat until mixture is smooth and fluffy. Pour into cooled pie crust. Refrigerate at least 2 hours before serving. Garnish with whipped cream and Chocolate Curls, or as desired. Store in refrigerator. 8 to 10 servings.

TIP: *To make individual tartlets, allow both pouches to stand at room temperature 15 to 20 minutes. Unfold crusts; sprinkle each with heaping teaspoon flour. Cut into 8 quarters. Place one quarter of prepared crust, floured side down, in bottom and up sides of tartlet pans. Trim edges. Generously prick crust with fork. Bake at 450°F. for 8 to 10 minutes until lightly browned; cool. Divide filling evenly into eight cooled tartlets.

NUTRITION INFORMATION PER SERVING

SERVING SIZE: 1/10 OF RECIPE		PERCENT U.S. RDA PER SERVING	
CALORIES	400	PROTEIN	8%
PROTEIN	5g	VITAMIN A	15%
CARBOHYDRATE	34g	VITAMIN C	*
FAT	28g	THIAMINE	2%
CHOLESTEROL	115mg	RIBOFLAVIN	10%
SODIUM	270mg	NIACIN	*
POTASSIUM	140mg	CALCIUM	2%
		IRON	8%

*Contains less than 2% of the U.S. RDA of this nutrient.

Choose this yummy cake for Valentine's Day or any other special day.

Chocolate Lovers' Cake

CAKE
1 pkg. Pillsbury Plus Devil's Food Cake Mix
1 cup dairy sour cream
¾ cup water
⅓ cup oil
3 eggs
4-oz. bar milk chocolate, grated

FILLING
21-oz. can cherry fruit pie filling
1 cup whipping cream, whipped, sweetened
¼ cup sliced almonds Chocolate Curls, if desired (see Index)

Heat oven to 350°F. Grease and flour two 9-inch round cake pans. In large bowl, combine cake mix, sour cream, water, oil and eggs at low speed until moistened; beat 2 minutes at **highest** speed. Gently fold in grated chocolate. Pour batter evenly into prepared pans. Bake at 350°F. for 35 to 45 minutes or until cake springs back when touched lightly in center. Cool 15 minutes; remove from pans. Cool completely.

Place 1 cake layer bottom side up on serving plate. Spoon or pipe 1 cup of whipped cream around top edge of cake. Spoon half of cherry filling over center of cake. Top with remaining cake layer bottom side down. Spoon remaining cherry filling in heart-shape over center of cake. Spoon or pipe remaining whipped cream around edge of heart. Garnish with almonds and additional Chocolate Curls. Store in refrigerator. 16 servings.

HIGH ALTITUDE—Above 3500 Feet: Add 3 tablespoons flour to dry cake mix. Bake at 375°F. for 30 to 40 minutes.

NUTRITION INFORMATION PER SERVING

SERVING SIZE: 1/16 OF RECIPE		PERCENT U.S. RDA PER SERVING	
CALORIES	400	PROTEIN	6%
PROTEIN	4g	VITAMIN A	10%
CARBOHYDRATE	47g	VITAMIN C	*
FAT	22g	THIAMINE	6%
CHOLESTEROL	80mg	RIBOFLAVIN	8%
SODIUM	290mg	NIACIN	4%
POTASSIUM	170mg	CALCIUM	10%
		IRON	6%

*Contains less than 2% of the U.S. RDA of this nutrient.

*This recipe from the 30th Bake-Off®
Contest is one of our most requested
recipes.*

Chocolate Mint
Parfait Bars

BASE
   1 pkg. Pillsbury Plus Devil's
      Food Cake Mix
   ⅓ cup margarine or butter,
      softened
   1 egg

FILLING
   1 envelope unflavored gelatin
   ¼ cup boiling water
   4 cups powdered sugar
   ½ cup margarine or butter,
      softened
   ½ cup shortening
   ¼ teaspoon peppermint extract
2 to 3 drops green food color

FROSTING
6-oz. pkg. (1 cup) semi-sweet
      chocolate chips
   3 tablespoons margarine or
      butter

Heat oven to 350°F. Grease 15x10-inch
jelly roll pan. In large bowl, combine
all base ingredients at low speed until
crumbly. Press into bottom of
prepared pan. Bake at 350°F. for
10 minutes. Cool completely.

Dissolve gelatin in boiling water; cool
slightly. In large bowl, combine
dissolved gelatin and 2 cups
powdered sugar. Add ½ cup
margarine, shortening, peppermint
extract and food color; beat 1 minute
at medium speed or until smooth and
creamy. Blend in remaining 2 cups
powdered sugar until smooth. Spread
filling evenly over cooled base.

In small saucepan over low heat, melt
chocolate chips and 3 tablespoons
margarine, stirring constantly until
well blended. Spoon frosting evenly
over filling, carefully spreading to
cover. Refrigerate until firm; cut into
bars. Let stand at room temperature
about 20 minutes before serving.
Store any remaining bars in
refrigerator. 48 bars.

HIGH ALTITUDE—Above 3500 Feet:
No change.

NUTRITION INFORMATION PER SERVING

SERVING SIZE: 1 BAR		PERCENT U.S. RDA PER SERVING	
CALORIES	160	PROTEIN	*
PROTEIN	1g	VITAMIN A	2%
CARBOHYDRATE	18g	VITAMIN C	*
FAT	9g	THIAMINE	*
CHOLESTEROL	6mg	RIBOFLAVIN	*
SODIUM	135mg	NIACIN	*
POTASSIUM	35mg	CALCIUM	2%
		IRON	*

*Contains less than 2% of the U.S. RDA of this nutrient.

*Pieces of angel food cake that are
scooped from the center of the cake
can make a quick English trifle.
Simply tear the cake into 1 to 2-inch
pieces and layer with sliced
strawberries, bananas and
whipped cream.*

Chocolate
Cream-Filled Angel
Food Dessert

CAKE
   1 (8-inch) prepared tube-shaped
      angel food cake

FILLING
   3 cups whipping cream
   1½ cups powdered sugar
   ¾ cup unsweetened cocoa

Slice 1 inch off top of cake; reserve. To
make a tunnel, slice down into cake
about 1 inch from inner and outer
edges. Scoop out cake within cuts,
leaving about 1 inch of cake to form a
base. (Use removed cake pieces for
another dessert.)

In large bowl, beat whipping cream,
powdered sugar and cocoa until stiff
peaks form. Fill tunnel of cake.
Replace top cake layer. Frost sides and
top. Garnish as desired. Store in
refrigerator. 16 servings.

NUTRITION INFORMATION PER SERVING

SERVING SIZE: 1/16 OF RECIPE		PERCENT U.S. RDA PER SERVING	
CALORIES	290	PROTEIN	6%
PROTEIN	4g	VITAMIN A	10%
CARBOHYDRATE	30g	VITAMIN C	*
FAT	17g	THIAMINE	2%
CHOLESTEROL	60mg	RIBOFLAVIN	8%
SODIUM	130mg	NIACIN	*
POTASSIUM	85mg	CALCIUM	2%
		IRON	4%

*Contains less than 2% of the U.S. RDA of this nutrient.

This Bake-Off® favorite has been revised somewhat over the years. It is an irresistible chocolate caramel bar.

Oatmeal Carmelitas

CRUST
- 2 cups Pillsbury's BEST® All Purpose or Unbleached Flour
- 2 cups quick-cooking rolled oats
- 1½ cups firmly packed brown sugar
- 1 teaspoon baking soda
- ½ teaspoon salt
- 1¼ cups margarine or butter, softened

FILLING
- 6-oz. pkg. (1 cup) semi-sweet chocolate chips
- ½ cup chopped nuts
- 12-oz. jar (1 cup) caramel ice cream topping
- 3 tablespoons flour

Heat oven to 350°F. Grease 13x9-inch pan. Lightly spoon flour into measuring cup; level off. In large bowl, combine all crust ingredients at low speed until crumbly. Press half of crumb mixture, about 3 cups, into bottom of prepared pan. Reserve remaining crumb mixture for topping. Bake at 350°F. for 10 minutes.

Sprinkle warm base with chocolate chips and nuts. Combine caramel topping and 3 tablespoons flour; drizzle evenly over chocolate chips and nuts. Sprinkle with reserved crumbs. Bake an additional 18 to 22 minutes or until golden brown. Cool completely. Refrigerate 1 to 2 hours; cut into bars. 36 bars.

HIGH ALTITUDE—Above 3500 Feet: No change.

NUTRITION INFORMATION PER SERVING

SERVING SIZE: 1 BAR		PERCENT U.S. RDA PER SERVING	
CALORIES	200	PROTEIN	2%
PROTEIN	2g	VITAMIN A	10%
CARBOHYDRATE	28g	VITAMIN C	*
FAT	9g	THIAMINE	10%
CHOLESTEROL	0mg	RIBOFLAVIN	4%
SODIUM	210mg	NIACIN	6%
POTASSIUM	90mg	CALCIUM	6%
		IRON	10%

*Contains less than 2% of the U.S. RDA of this nutrient.

Delectable and fudgy, this brownie has a marbling of cream cheese.

Zebra Brownies

FILLING
- 2 (3-oz.) pkg. cream cheese, softened
- ¼ cup sugar
- ½ teaspoon vanilla
- 1 egg

BROWNIES
- 21½-oz. pkg. Pillsbury Family Size Deluxe Fudge Brownie Mix
- ⅓ cup very hot tap water
- ⅓ cup oil
- 1 egg

Heat oven to 350°F. Generously grease bottom only of 13x9-inch pan. In small bowl, beat all filling ingredients until smooth; set aside. In large bowl, combine all brownie ingredients; beat 50 strokes with spoon. Spread half of batter in prepared pan. Pour cream cheese mixture over batter, spreading to cover. Place spoonfuls of remaining batter on top of cream cheese. Marble by pulling knife through batter in wide curves; turn pan and repeat.

Bake at 350°F. for 30 to 35 minutes or until set. DO NOT OVERBAKE. Cool completely. Refrigerate at least 1 hour; cut into bars. Store in refrigerator. 36 bars.

HIGH ALTITUDE—Above 3500 Feet: Add 2 tablespoons flour to dry brownie mix. Bake as directed above.

NUTRITION INFORMATION PER SERVING

SERVING SIZE: 1 BAR		PERCENT U.S. RDA PER SERVING	
CALORIES	110	PROTEIN	2%
PROTEIN	1g	VITAMIN A	*
CARBOHYDRATE	15g	VITAMIN C	*
FAT	5g	THIAMINE	2%
CHOLESTEROL	20mg	RIBOFLAVIN	2%
SODIUM	80mg	NIACIN	*
POTASSIUM	30mg	CALCIUM	*
		IRON	2%

*Contains less than 2% of the U.S. RDA of this nutrient.

This recipe remains popular year after year. The filling will bake up between the layers creating a creamy ribbon.

Double Fudge Fancifill

FILLING
1/4 cup sugar
1 tablespoon cornstarch
8-oz. pkg. cream cheese, softened
2 tablespoons margarine or butter, softened
2 tablespoons milk
1/2 teaspoon vanilla
1 egg

CAKE
1 pkg. Pillsbury Plus Devil's Food Cake Mix
1 cup water
1/3 cup oil
3 eggs

FROSTING
1 can Pillsbury Ready To Spread Chocolate Fudge Frosting Supreme

Heat oven to 350°F. Grease and flour 13x9-inch pan. In small bowl, combine all filling ingredients; beat at highest speed until smooth and creamy. Set aside. In large bowl, combine all cake ingredients and beat at low speed until moistened. Beat 2 minutes at **highest** speed. Pour half of batter into prepared pan. Pour filling mixture over batter; spread carefully to cover. Pour remaining batter evenly over filling.

Bake at 350°F. for 45 to 55 minutes or until toothpick inserted in center comes out clean. Cool completely. Frost; garnish as desired. Cover; store in refrigerator. 16 servings.

HIGH ALTITUDE—Above 3500 Feet: Omit milk in filling. Add 1/4 cup flour to dry cake mix. Bake at 375°F. for 35 to 45 minutes.

NUTRITION INFORMATION PER SERVING

SERVING SIZE: 1/16 OF RECIPE		PERCENT U.S. RDA PER SERVING	
CALORIES	390	PROTEIN	6%
PROTEIN	4g	VITAMIN A	6%
CARBOHYDRATE	45g	VITAMIN C	*
FAT	21g	THIAMINE	6%
CHOLESTEROL	80mg	RIBOFLAVIN	6%
SODIUM	410mg	NIACIN	2%
POTASSIUM	140mg	CALCIUM	10%
		IRON	6%

*Contains less than 2% of the U.S. RDA of this nutrient.

This recipe was developed for those of you requesting an easy cookie made from a cake mix. The cookies puff during baking and when removed from the oven settle to form a pretty crinkled top.

German Chocolate Cake Mix Cookies

1 pkg. Pillsbury Plus German Chocolate Cake Mix
6-oz. pkg. (1 cup) semi-sweet chocolate chips
1/2 cup rolled oats
1/2 cup raisins
1/2 cup margarine or butter, melted
2 eggs, slightly beaten

Heat oven to 350°F. In large bowl, combine all ingredients; blend well. Drop dough by rounded teaspoonful 2 inches apart on ungreased cookie sheets. Bake at 350°F. for 8 to 10 minutes or until set. Cool 1 minute; remove from cookie sheets. 6 dozen cookies.

HIGH ALTITUDE—Above 3500 Feet: Add 2 tablespoons flour to dry cake mix. Bake as directed above.

NUTRITION INFORMATION PER SERVING

SERVING SIZE: 1 COOKIE		PERCENT U.S. RDA PER SERVING	
CALORIES	60	PROTEIN	*
PROTEIN	1g	VITAMIN A	*
CARBOHYDRATE	8g	VITAMIN C	*
FAT	3g	THIAMINE	2%
CHOLESTEROL	8mg	RIBOFLAVIN	*
SODIUM	75mg	NIACIN	*
POTASSIUM	25mg	CALCIUM	*
		IRON	2%

*Contains less than 2% of the U.S. RDA of this nutrient.

German Chocolate Cake Mix Cookies

When this recipe won a prize in the Bake-Off® Contest, it was made with a frosting mix that is no longer available. Because of its great popularity, the recipe has been revised to make the fudgy tunnel from scratch.

Tunnel of Fudge Cake

CAKE
- 1¾ cups margarine or butter, softened
- 1¾ cups granulated sugar
- 6 eggs
- 2 cups powdered sugar
- 2¼ cups Pillsbury's BEST® All Purpose or Unbleached Flour
- ¾ cup unsweetened cocoa
- 2 cups chopped walnuts*

GLAZE
- ¾ cup powdered sugar
- ¼ cup unsweetened cocoa
- 1½ to 2 tablespoons milk

Heat oven to 350°F. Grease and flour 12-cup fluted tube pan or 10-inch tube pan. In large bowl, beat margarine and granulated sugar until light and fluffy. Add eggs one at a time, beating well after each addition. Gradually add powdered sugar; blend well. Lightly spoon flour into measuring cup; level off. By hand, stir in remaining cake ingredients until well blended. Spoon batter into prepared pan; spread evenly. Bake at 350°F. for 58 to 62 minutes.** Cool upright in pan on wire rack 1 hour; invert onto serving plate. Cool completely.

In small bowl, combine all glaze ingredients until well blended. Spoon over top of cake, allowing some to run down sides. Store tightly covered. 16 servings.

TIPS: *Nuts are essential for the success of this recipe.

**Since this cake has a soft tunnel of fudge, an ordinary doneness test cannot be used. Accurate oven temperature and bake time are critical.

HIGH ALTITUDE—Above 3500 Feet: Increase flour to 2¼ cups plus 3 tablespoons. Bake as directed above.

NUTRITION INFORMATION PER SERVING

SERVING SIZE: 1/16 OF RECIPE		PERCENT U.S. RDA PER SERVING	
CALORIES	550	PROTEIN	10%
PROTEIN	7g	VITAMIN A	20%
CARBOHYDRATE	58g	VITAMIN C	*
FAT	33g	THIAMINE	15%
CHOLESTEROL	100mg	RIBOFLAVIN	10%
SODIUM	300mg	NIACIN	6%
POTASSIUM	170mg	CALCIUM	8%
		IRON	10%

*Contains less than 2% of the U.S. RDA of this nutrient.

Rich, creamy, delicious and so easy with only six ingredients.

Six-Layer Bars

- ½ cup margarine or butter
- 1½ cups graham cracker crumbs
- 1 cup chopped nuts
- 6-oz. pkg. (1 cup) semi-sweet chocolate chips
- 1½ cups coconut
- 14-oz. can sweetened condensed milk

Heat oven to 350°F. In 13x9-inch pan, melt margarine while heating oven. Combine crumbs with margarine; press into bottom of pan. Sprinkle with nuts, chocolate chips and coconut. Pour sweetened condensed milk over mixture. Bake at 350°F. for 20 to 30 minutes or until lightly browned. Cool; cut into bars. 36 bars.

NUTRITION INFORMATION PER SERVING

SERVING SIZE: 1 BAR		PERCENT U.S. RDA PER SERVING	
CALORIES	140	PROTEIN	2%
PROTEIN	2g	VITAMIN A	2%
CARBOHYDRATE	14g	VITAMIN C	*
FAT	9g	THIAMINE	*
CHOLESTEROL	4mg	RIBOFLAVIN	4%
SODIUM	70mg	NIACIN	*
POTASSIUM	100mg	CALCIUM	4%
		IRON	2%

*Contains less than 2% of the U.S. RDA of this nutrient.

One of the most popular three-layer bars ever!

Rocky Road Fudge Bars

BASE
- ½ cup margarine or butter
- 1 oz. (1 square) unsweetened chocolate, chopped
- 1 cup Pillsbury's BEST® All Purpose or Unbleached Flour
- 1 cup sugar
- 1 teaspoon baking powder
- 1 teaspoon vanilla
- 2 eggs
- ¾ cup chopped nuts

FILLING
- 8-oz. pkg. cream cheese, softened, reserving 2 oz. for frosting
- ¼ cup margarine or butter, softened
- ½ cup sugar
- 2 tablespoons flour
- ½ teaspoon vanilla
- 1 egg
- ¼ cup chopped nuts
- 6-oz. pkg. (1 cup) semi-sweet chocolate chips

FROSTING
- 2 cups miniature marshmallows
- ¼ cup margarine or butter
- ¼ cup milk
- 1 oz. (1 square) unsweetened chocolate, chopped
- Reserved 2 oz. cream cheese
- 3 cups powdered sugar, sifted
- 1 teaspoon vanilla

Heat oven to 350°F. Grease and flour 13x9-inch pan. In large saucepan over low heat, melt ½ cup margarine and 1 oz. unsweetened chocolate, stirring constantly until smooth. Lightly spoon flour into measuring cup; level off. Add 1 cup flour and remaining base ingredients; mix well. Spread into prepared pan.

In small bowl, combine all filling ingredients except ¼ cup nuts and chocolate chips. Beat 1 minute at medium speed until smooth and fluffy; stir in nuts. Spread over chocolate mixture; sprinkle evenly with chocolate chips. Bake at 350°F. for 25 to 35 minutes or until toothpick inserted in center comes out clean.

Immediately sprinkle marshmallows over top. Return to oven and bake an additional 2 minutes. In large saucepan over low heat, combine ¼ cup margarine, milk, 1 oz. unsweetened chocolate and reserved 2 oz. cream cheese; stir until well blended. Remove from heat; stir in powdered sugar and 1 teaspoon vanilla until smooth. Immediately pour frosting over marshmallows and lightly swirl with knife to marble. Refrigerate until firm; cut into bars. 48 bars.

HIGH ALTITUDE—Above 3500 Feet: No change.

NUTRITION INFORMATION PER SERVING

SERVING SIZE: 1 BAR		PERCENT U.S. RDA PER SERVING	
CALORIES	160	PROTEIN	2%
PROTEIN	2g	VITAMIN A	4%
CARBOHYDRATE	19g	VITAMIN C	*
FAT	9g	THIAMINE	2%
CHOLESTEROL	20mg	RIBOFLAVIN	2%
SODIUM	70mg	NIACIN	*
POTASSIUM	50mg	CALCIUM	2%
		IRON	2%

*Contains less than 2% of the U.S. RDA of this nutrient.

This cookie takes the shape of the surprise chocolate mint in the center. They are great to enjoy with a cup of coffee.

Starlight Mint Surprise Cookies

~~~

   1 cup sugar
   ½ cup firmly packed brown
      sugar
   ¾ cup margarine or butter,
      softened
   2 eggs
   2 tablespoons water
   1 teaspoon vanilla
   3 cups Pillsbury's BEST® All
      Purpose or Unbleached
      Flour
   1 teaspoon baking soda
   ½ teaspoon salt
2 (6-oz.) pkg. solid chocolate mint
      candy wafers, unwrapped
  60 nut halves

In large bowl, combine sugar, brown sugar, margarine, eggs, water and vanilla; mix well. Lightly spoon flour into measuring cup; level off. Stir in flour, soda and salt; mix well. Chill dough at least 2 hours.

Heat oven to 375°F. Enclose each wafer completely in about 1 tablespoonful of dough; place 2 inches apart on ungreased cookie sheets. Top each with nut half. Bake at 375°F. for 7 to 9 minutes or until light golden brown. 5 dozen cookies.

HIGH ALTITUDE—Above 3500 Feet: No change.

NUTRITION INFORMATION PER SERVING

SERVING SIZE: 1 COOKIE		PERCENT U.S. RDA PER SERVING	
CALORIES	100	PROTEIN	*
PROTEIN	1g	VITAMIN A	2%
CARBOHYDRATE	13g	VITAMIN C	*
FAT	5g	THIAMINE	2%
CHOLESTEROL	8mg	RIBOFLAVIN	*
SODIUM	65mg	NIACIN	*
POTASSIUM	40mg	CALCIUM	*
		IRON	2%

*Contains less than 2% of the U.S. RDA of this nutrient.

This Bake-Off® Contest winner puts together chocolate and nuts in a rich brown sugar cookie mixture for an entertaining and unusual shape.

Snappy Turtle Cookies

COOKIES

- ½ cup firmly packed brown sugar
- ½ cup margarine or butter, softened
- ¼ teaspoon vanilla
- ⅛ teaspoon maple flavoring, if desired
- 1 egg
- 1 egg, separated
- 1½ cups Pillsbury's BEST® All Purpose or Unbleached Flour
- ¼ teaspoon baking soda
- ¼ teaspoon salt
- 1½ to 2 cups split pecan halves

FROSTING

- ⅓ cup semi-sweet chocolate chips
- 3 tablespoons milk
- 1 tablespoon margarine or butter
- 1 cup powdered sugar

In medium bowl, beat brown sugar and ½ cup margarine until light and fluffy. Add vanilla, maple flavoring, 1 whole egg and 1 egg yolk; beat well. Lightly spoon flour into measuring cup; level off. Stir in flour, baking soda and salt; mix well. Refrigerate dough for easier handling.

Heat oven to 350°F. Grease cookie sheets. Arrange pecan pieces in groups of 5 on prepared cookie sheets to resemble head and legs of turtle. Beat 1 reserved egg white. Shape rounded teaspoonful of dough into balls. Dip bottoms into egg white and press lightly onto pecans. (Tips of pecans should show.) Bake at 350°F. for 10 to 12 minutes or until light golden brown around edges. DO NOT OVERBAKE. Remove from cookie sheets immediately. Cool.

In small saucepan over low heat, combine chocolate chips, milk and 1 tablespoon margarine over low heat; stir until smooth. Remove from heat; stir in powdered sugar. If necessary, add additional powdered sugar for spreading consistency. Frost cookies. 3½ dozen cookies.

HIGH ALTITUDE—Above 3500 Feet: No change.

NUTRITION INFORMATION PER SERVING

SERVING SIZE: 1 COOKIE		PERCENT U.S. RDA PER SERVING	
CALORIES	110	PROTEIN	*
PROTEIN	1g	VITAMIN A	2%
CARBOHYDRATE	10g	VITAMIN C	*
FAT	7g	THIAMINE	4%
CHOLESTEROL	10mg	RIBOFLAVIN	*
SODIUM	50mg	NIACIN	*
POTASSIUM	45mg	CALCIUM	*
		IRON	2%

*Contains less than 2% of the U.S. RDA of this nutrient.

COOK'S NOTE

What is the gray discoloration found on chocolate?

This is called "bloom." When chocolate is stored at temperatures above 78°F. it melts, causing the cocoa butter to rise to the surface. This is called "cocoa butter bloom." When condensation causes sugar to dissolve and rise to the surface, it is called "sugar bloom."

Bloom does not affect the flavor or quality of chocolate and when used in a recipe, it will regain its original color. To prevent bloom, store chocolate tightly covered in a cool, dry place.

For a little variety, try chunks of chocolate in place of chocolate chips—see tip below for directions.

Chocolate Chip Cookies

¾ cup firmly packed brown sugar
½ cup sugar
½ cup margarine or butter, softened
½ cup shortening
1½ teaspoons vanilla
1 egg
1¾ cups Pillsbury's BEST® All Purpose or Unbleached Flour
1 teaspoon baking soda
½ teaspoon salt
6-oz. pkg. (1 cup) semi-sweet chocolate chips
½ cup chopped nuts or sunflower nuts, if desired

Heat oven to 375°F. In large bowl, beat brown sugar, sugar, margarine and shortening until light and fluffy. Add vanilla and egg; beat well. Lightly spoon flour into measuring cup; level off. Add flour, baking soda and salt; mix well. Stir in chocolate chips and nuts. Drop dough by teaspoonful 2 inches apart onto ungreased cookie sheets. Bake at 375°F. for 8 to 10 minutes or until light golden brown. Cool 1 minute; remove from cookie sheets. 4 dozen cookies.

TIP: To make Chocolate Chunk Cookies, substitute 8 oz. coarsely chopped semi-sweet chocolate for chocolate chips. Drop dough by tablespoonful 3 inches apart onto ungreased cookie sheets. Bake at 375°F. for 9 to 12 minutes or until light golden brown. 3 dozen cookies.

HIGH ALTITUDE—Above 3500 Feet: No change.

NUTRITION INFORMATION PER SERVING

SERVING SIZE: COOKIE		PERCENT U.S. RDA PER SERVING	
CALORIES	100	PROTEIN	*
PROTEIN	1g	VITAMIN A	*
CARBOHYDRATE	11g	VITAMIN C	*
FAT	6g	THIAMINE	2%
CHOLESTEROL	6mg	RIBOFLAVIN	*
SODIUM	70mg	NIACIN	*
POTASSIUM	40mg	CALCIUM	*
		IRON	2%

*Contains less than 2% of the U.S. RDA of this nutrient.

This recipe makes two scrumptious 9-inch pies. Enjoy one immediately and save the other one for another occasion.

Brownie Sundae Pies

BROWNIES
22½-oz. pkg. Pillsbury Deluxe Fudge Brownie Mix
½ cup very hot tap water
½ cup oil
2 eggs

TOPPING
12-oz. jar (1 cup) fudge ice cream topping
½ gallon butter brickle or any flavor ice cream

Heat oven to 325°F. Grease two 9-inch pie pans. In large bowl, combine all brownie ingredients; beat 50 strokes with spoon. Pour batter into prepared pans. Bake at 325°F. for 20 to 25 minutes. DO NOT OVERBAKE. Cool completely.

Spread ⅓ cup ice cream topping on top of each brownie layer. Overlap large spoonfuls of ice cream to cover top; place in freezer. In small saucepan over low heat, soften remaining ice cream topping. Drizzle over ice cream. Cover; freeze several hours or overnight. Let stand at room temperature about 5 to 10 minutes before serving. 2 pies; 8 servings each.

HIGH ALTITUDE—Above 3500 Feet: Add 2 tablespoons flour to dry brownie mix. Bake at 325°F. for 25 to 30 minutes.

NUTRITION INFORMATION PER SERVING

SERVING SIZE: 1/16 OF RECIPE		PERCENT U.S. RDA PER SERVING	
CALORIES	450	PROTEIN	8%
PROTEIN	5g	VITAMIN A	6%
CARBOHYDRATE	58g	VITAMIN C	*
FAT	22g	THIAMINE	6%
CHOLESTEROL	60mg	RIBOFLAVIN	15%
SODIUM	210mg	NIACIN	4%
POTASSIUM	180mg	CALCIUM	8%
		IRON	4%

*Contains less than 2% of the U.S. RDA of this nutrient.

Pictured top to bottom: *Heavenly Chocolate Brownie Cookies p. 26,*
Chocolate Chunk Pecan Brownies p. 25.

Cookies & Bars

Cookies & Bars

The best in bite-sized

With December's confections now a mere memory, we offer a chapter brimming with edible suggestions for conquering those post-holiday blahs. Set your kitchen humming by stirring up several batches of tempting cookies, brownies, snaps or bars. After filling the cookie jar, you can pop extras in the freezer or share a plateful with a neighbor—a wonderful way to express "Happy New Year" greetings! Go a step further and team these freshly baked goodies with one of our toasty microwaved drinks found in Chapter Five. Certainly a reward to relish after a busy day at school or work or to greet an unexpected visitor.

And it's no wonder cookies and bars are so popular. They are quickly prepared, simple to serve, easy to eat and most can be toted and mailed with excellent results. This seductive sampling features flavors and textures to satisfy all ages and tastes and preparation steps to suit all skill levels.

Cookies for a centerpiece or special gift? You bet! Just take a peek at the intriguing Valentine Heart Bouquet. Heart-shaped, frosted cookies, cleverly arranged in a pretty vase with complementary ribbons and frothy baby's breath, can be a festive focal point for a special Valentine's Day dinner, an engagement celebration, a wedding shower, an anniversary reception or a magical candlelight dinner for two. And for a unique Valentine's Day greeting, wrap them in a gift box.

These marvelous, tender, chocolate-dipped cookies with the tangy essence of orange melt in your mouth. With waxed paper between layers, store cookies in a covered container.

Orange Butter Cookies in Chocolate

COOKIE
- 1 cup sugar
- ¾ cup butter, softened
- 1 teaspoon vanilla
- 1 egg
- 2 cups Pillsbury's BEST® All Purpose or Unbleached Flour
- 1 teaspoon baking powder
- ¾ teaspoon salt
- 2 tablespoons grated orange peel

GLAZE
- 6-oz. pkg. (1 cup) semi-sweet chocolate chips
- ¼ cup shortening
- 3 tablespoons light corn syrup

Heat oven to 375°F. In large bowl, beat sugar and butter until light and fluffy. Add vanilla and egg; blend well. Lightly spoon flour into measuring cup; level off. Stir in flour, baking powder, salt and orange peel. Roll dough into 1-inch balls. Place 2 inches apart on ungreased cookie sheets. Flatten with bottom of glass dipped in sugar to ⅛ to ¼-inch thickness. Bake at 375°F. for 6 to 8 minutes or until edges are lightly browned. Cool 1 minute; remove from cookie sheets.

In small saucepan over low heat, combine glaze ingredients, stirring constantly until smooth. Remove from heat. Pour glaze into glass measuring cup; set in pan of hot water. Dip ½ of each cookie into glaze; shake off excess chocolate. Place dipped cookies on waxed paper-lined cookie sheets. Chill until glaze is set, about 10 minutes. 6 dozen cookies.

HIGH ALTITUDE—Above 3500 Feet:
No change.

NUTRITION INFORMATION PER SERVING

SERVING SIZE: 1 COOKIE		PERCENT U.S. RDA PER SERVING	
CALORIES	70	PROTEIN	*
PROTEIN	1g	VITAMIN A	*
CARBOHYDRATE	7g	VITAMIN C	*
FAT	4g	THIAMINE	*
CHOLESTEROL	8mg	RIBOFLAVIN	*
SODIUM	50mg	NIACIN	*
POTASSIUM	15mg	CALCIUM	*
		IRON	*

*Contains less than 2% of the U.S. RDA of this nutrient.

This culinary inspiration was developed for chocoholics. A moist, nut-textured, intensely flavored brownie to satisfy that chocolate craving...at least for a little while.

Chocolate Chunk Pecan Brownies

- 1 cup margarine or butter
- 2 cups sugar
- 2 teaspoons vanilla
- 4 eggs, slightly beaten
- 1 cup Pillsbury's BEST® All Purpose or Unbleached Flour
- ½ cup unsweetened cocoa
- ½ teaspoon salt
- 8 oz. (8 squares) semi-sweet chocolate, coarsely chopped
- 1 cup chopped pecans

Heat oven to 350°F. Grease 13x9-inch pan. In medium saucepan over low heat, melt margarine. Add sugar, vanilla and eggs; blend well. Lightly spoon flour into measuring cup; level off. Stir in flour, cocoa and salt; mix well. Add chocolate and pecans. Pour into prepared pan. Bake at 350°F. for 30 to 40 minutes or until set. Cool; cut into bars. 36 bars.

HIGH ALTITUDE—Above 3500 Feet:
No change.

NUTRITION INFORMATION PER SERVING

SERVING SIZE: 1 BAR		PERCENT U.S. RDA PER SERVING	
CALORIES	170	PROTEIN	2%
PROTEIN	2g	VITAMIN A	4%
CARBOHYDRATE	19g	VITAMIN C	*
FAT	10g	THIAMINE	4%
CHOLESTEROL	30mg	RIBOFLAVIN	2%
SODIUM	105mg	NIACIN	*
POTASSIUM	55mg	CALCIUM	*
		IRON	2%

*Contains less than 2% of the U.S. RDA of this nutrient.

Probably one of the best little cookies you'll ever eat. This recipe requires the use of parchment paper which is readily available at a supermarket or specialty food store.

Heavenly Chocolate Brownie Cookies
〰️

4 oz. (4 squares) semi-sweet chocolate, chopped
2 oz. (2 squares) unsweetened chocolate, chopped
⅓ cup margarine or butter
¾ cup sugar
1½ teaspoons instant coffee granules
2 eggs
½ cup Pillsbury's BEST® All Purpose or Unbleached Flour
¼ teaspoon baking powder
¼ teaspoon salt
¾ cup milk chocolate chips
¾ cup chopped walnuts

Heat oven to 350°F. Cover cookie sheets with parchment paper. In small saucepan over low heat, melt semi-sweet chocolate, unsweetened chocolate and margarine, stirring constantly until smooth. Remove from heat; cool. In large bowl, beat sugar, instant coffee and eggs at highest speed for 2 to 3 minutes. Blend in melted chocolate. Lightly spoon flour into measuring cup; level off. Stir in flour, baking powder and salt; mix well. Stir in milk chocolate chips and walnuts; mix well.

Drop dough by teaspoonful 2 inches apart onto prepared cookie sheets. Bake at 350°F. for 7 to 11 minutes or until tops of cookies are cracked. DO NOT OVERBAKE. Cool 1 minute; remove from parchment paper. 3 dozen cookies.

HIGH ALTITUDE—Above 3500 Feet: No change.

NUTRITION INFORMATION PER SERVING

SERVING SIZE: 1 COOKIE		PERCENT U.S. RDA PER SERVING	
CALORIES	110	PROTEIN	2%
PROTEIN	1g	VITAMIN A	*
CARBOHYDRATE	10g	VITAMIN C	*
FAT	7g	THIAMINE	*
CHOLESTEROL	15mg	RIBOFLAVIN	*
SODIUM	40mg	NIACIN	*
POTASSIUM	55mg	CALCIUM	*
		IRON	2%

*Contains less than 2% of the U.S. RDA of this nutrient.

The flavor is delectable in this tender, shaped cookie with a surprise chunk of creamy white chocolate in the center. What a treat!

White Capped Mocha Cookies
〰️

COOKIE
½ cup firmly packed brown sugar
¼ cup sugar
½ cup margarine or butter, softened
8-oz. pkg. cream cheese, softened, reserving 2 oz. for frosting
2 teaspoons instant coffee
2 teaspoons hot water
1 egg
2 cups Pillsbury's BEST® All Purpose or Unbleached Flour
¼ cup unsweetened cocoa
1 teaspoon baking powder

FILLING
2 to 3 oz. vanilla-flavored candy coating or white chocolate, cut into small pieces (about ¼-inch cubes)

FROSTING
1 cup powdered sugar
Reserved 2 oz. cream cheese, softened
2 to 3 teaspoons milk

Heat oven to 350°F. In large bowl, beat brown sugar, sugar, margarine and 6 oz. cream cheese until light and fluffy. Dissolve instant coffee in hot water. Add dissolved coffee and egg; blend well. Lightly spoon flour into measuring cup; level off. Add flour, cocoa and baking powder; mix well.

Shape one level tablespoon dough around a small chunk of candy coating, covering completely. Place 2 inches apart on cookie sheets. Bake at 350°F. for 8 to 11 minutes. Cool.

In small bowl, blend frosting ingredients, adding 1 teaspoon milk at a time for desired consistency. Frost cooled cookies. 4½ dozen cookies.

HIGH ALTITUDE—Above 3500 Feet: Decrease baking powder to ½ teaspoon. Bake as directed above.

NUTRITION INFORMATION PER SERVING

SERVING SIZE: COOKIE		PERCENT U.S. RDA PER SERVING	
CALORIES	100	PROTEIN	*
PROTEIN	1g	VITAMIN A	2%
CARBOHYDRATE	10g	VITAMIN C	*
FAT	4g	THIAMINE	2%
CHOLESTEROL	10mg	RIBOFLAVIN	*
SODIUM	45mg	NIACIN	*
POTASSIUM	30mg	CALCIUM	2%
		IRON	2%

Contains less than 2% of the U.S. RDA of this nutrient.

A classic butterscotch brownie deliciously laced with milk chocolate chips in the bar and a creamy milk chocolate frosting. The butterscotch and milk chocolate flavors complement each other nicely.

Butterscotch Milk Chocolate Chip Bars

BAR
- 1 ½ cups firmly packed brown sugar
- ½ cup margarine or butter, softened
- 2 teaspoons vanilla
- 2 eggs
- 2 cups Pillsbury's BEST® All Purpose or Unbleached Flour
- 2 teaspoons baking powder
- ½ teaspoon salt
- 11.5-oz. pkg. (1⅞ cups) milk chocolate chips, reserving 1 cup for frosting
- ½ cup chopped nuts, if desired

FROSTING
- Reserved 1 cup milk chocolate chips
- ¼ cup margarine or butter
- 1 ¼ cups powdered sugar
- Dash salt
- 3 tablespoons milk
- 1 teaspoon vanilla

Heat oven to 350°F. Grease 13x9-inch pan. In large bowl, beat brown sugar and ½ cup margarine until light and fluffy. Add 2 teaspoons vanilla and eggs; blend well. Lightly spoon flour into measuring cup; level off. Add flour, baking powder and ½ teaspoon salt; mix well. Add ⅞ cup milk chocolate chips and nuts. Spread into prepared pan. Bake at 350°F. for 15 to 20 minutes or until edges are light brown. DO NOT OVERBAKE. Cool.

In small saucepan over low heat, melt 1 cup milk chocolate chips and ¼ cup margarine, stirring constantly until smooth. Remove from heat. Add powdered sugar, dash salt, milk and 1 teaspoon vanilla; blend well. Spread over cooled bars. Cut into bars. 36 bars.

HIGH ALTITUDE—Above 3500 Feet: No change.

NUTRITION INFORMATION PER SERVING

SERVING SIZE: 1 BAR		PERCENT U.S. RDA PER SERVING	
CALORIES	170	PROTEIN	2%
PROTEIN	2g	VITAMIN A	2%
CARBOHYDRATE	23g	VITAMIN C	*
FAT	8g	THIAMINE	4%
CHOLESTEROL	15mg	RIBOFLAVIN	2%
SODIUM	100mg	NIACIN	2%
POTASSIUM	85mg	CALCIUM	4%
		IRON	4%

*Contains less than 2% of the U.S. RDA of this nutrient.

Kahlua Buttercream-Filled Cookie Cups

COOKIE
1/3 cup sugar
1/2 cup butter, softened
1/2 teaspoon vanilla
1/8 teaspoon almond extract
1 egg yolk
1 cup Pillsbury's BEST® All Purpose or Unbleached Flour
Dash salt

FILLING
2 tablespoons unsweetened cocoa
1/2 cup butter, softened
1 cup powdered sugar
2 tablespoons coffee-flavored liqueur
Grated Chocolate (see Index)

Heat oven to 350°F. Grease 24 miniature muffin cups or 1 1/2-inch tartlet tins. In small bowl, beat sugar and 1/2 cup butter until light and fluffy. Add vanilla, almond extract and egg yolk; blend well. Lightly spoon flour into measuring cup; level off. Stir in flour and salt; mix well. Chill dough 1 hour for easier handling.

Place about 2 teaspoons dough into prepared muffin cups; press dough into bottom and up sides to form shells. Bake at 350°F. for 10 to 15 minutes or until light golden brown. Very carefully remove from muffin cups; cool.

In small bowl, beat cocoa and 1/2 cup butter until light and fluffy. Add powdered sugar and liqueur; blend well. Spoon filling into pastry bag with desired decorating tip; pipe filling into cookie cups. Sprinkle with Grated Chocolate. Store in refrigerator. 2 dozen cookie cups.

HIGH ALTITUDE—Above 3500 Feet: Decrease butter in cookie to 7 tablespoons. Bake as directed above.

NUTRITION INFORMATION PER SERVING

SERVING SIZE: 1 COOKIE CUP		PERCENT U.S. RDA PER SERVING	
CALORIES	130	PROTEIN	*
PROTEIN	1g	VITAMIN A	6%
CARBOHYDRATE	13g	VITAMIN C	*
FAT	8g	THIAMINE	2%
CHOLESTEROL	30mg	RIBOFLAVIN	*
SODIUM	85mg	NIACIN	*
POTASSIUM	15mg	CALCIUM	*
		IRON	2%

*Contains less than 2% of the U.S. RDA of this nutrient.

One of the taste panel's favorite chocolate recipes.

Fudgy Caramel Wedges

BAR
2 oz. (2 squares) semi-sweet chocolate, chopped
1 oz. (1 square) unsweetened chocolate, chopped
1/2 cup margarine or butter
3/4 cup Pillsbury's BEST® All Purpose or Unbleached Flour
3/4 cup sugar
1 tablespoon vanilla
2 eggs
1/2 cup coarsely chopped pecans

TOPPING
10 vanilla caramels, unwrapped
2 tablespoons milk
1/2 oz. (1/2 square) unsweetened chocolate, chopped
2 teaspoons margarine or butter
1 teaspoon light corn syrup

Heat oven to 325°F. Line 9-inch round cake pan with foil; grease. In medium saucepan over low heat, melt 2 oz. semi-sweet chocolate, 1 oz. unsweetened chocolate and 1/2 cup margarine, stirring constantly. Cool slightly. Lightly spoon flour into measuring cup; level off. Add flour, sugar, vanilla and eggs; blend well. Pour into prepared pan. Sprinkle nuts over batter. Bake at 325°F. for 20 to 30 minutes or until set.

In small saucepan over low heat, melt caramels and milk, stirring frequently until smooth. Drizzle over bars. In same saucepan over low heat, melt 1/2 oz. unsweetened chocolate, 2 teaspoons margarine and corn syrup. Drizzle over bars. Cool completely; cut into wedges. 12 to 16 servings.

HIGH ALTITUDE—Above 3500 Feet: Decrease sugar by 1 tablespoon. Bake at 350°F. for 20 to 30 minutes.

NUTRITION INFORMATION PER SERVING

SERVING SIZE: 1/16 OF RECIPE		PERCENT U.S. RDA PER SERVING	
CALORIES	210	PROTEIN	2%
PROTEIN	2g	VITAMIN A	6%
CARBOHYDRATE	22g	VITAMIN C	*
FAT	13g	THIAMINE	4%
CHOLESTEROL	35mg	RIBOFLAVIN	4%
SODIUM	95mg	NIACIN	2%
POTASSIUM	80mg	CALCIUM	2%
		IRON	4%

*Contains less than 2% of the U.S. RDA of this nutrient.

Fudgy Caramel Wedges

The use of chocolate syrup makes this cake-like textured brownie deliciously easy.

Chocolate Syrup Pecan Brownies

BAR

   1 cup sugar
   ½ cup margarine or butter, softened
   1 tablespoon vanilla
   3 eggs
16-oz. can chocolate-flavored syrup
   1¼ cups Pillsbury's BEST® All Purpose or Unbleached Flour
   ½ cup finely chopped nuts

FROSTING

   ¼ cup margarine or butter
   ¼ cup unsweetened cocoa
   1½ cups powdered sugar
   2½ tablespoons milk
   ½ teaspoon vanilla
   ½ cup finely chopped nuts

Heat oven to 350°F. Grease 13x9-inch pan. In large bowl, beat sugar and ½ cup margarine until light and fluffy. Add 1 tablespoon vanilla, eggs and chocolate syrup; blend well. Lightly spoon flour into measuring cup; level off. Stir in flour; mix well. Add ½ cup chopped nuts. Pour into prepared pan. Bake at 350°F. for 30 to 35 minutes. Cool.

In medium saucepan over medium heat, melt ¼ cup margarine. Blend in cocoa and heat just until mixture comes to a boil, stirring constantly; cool. Blend in powdered sugar, milk and ½ teaspoon vanilla until smooth. Stir in ½ cup nuts. Spread carefully over cooled bars. Cut into bars. 36 bars.

HIGH ALTITUDE—Above 3500 Feet: No change.

NUTRITION INFORMATION PER SERVING

SERVING SIZE: 1 BAR		PERCENT U.S. RDA PER SERVING	
CALORIES	160	PROTEIN	2%
PROTEIN	2g	VITAMIN A	2%
CARBOHYDRATE	22g	VITAMIN C	*
FAT	7g	THIAMINE	2%
CHOLESTEROL	25mg	RIBOFLAVIN	2%
SODIUM	60mg	NIACIN	*
POTASSIUM	70mg	CALCIUM	2%
		IRON	2%

*Contains less than 2% of the U.S. RDA of this nutrient.

The almond paste gives this bar a velvety texture and fantastic flavor.

Almond Fudge Brownies

BROWNIES

   1 teaspoon instant coffee
   2 tablespoons hot water
6-oz. pkg. (1 cup) semi-sweet chocolate chips
   4 eggs, separated
   1 cup sugar
   ½ cup margarine or butter, softened
3½-oz. pkg. almond paste, crumbled into small pieces
   1 cup Pillsbury's BEST® All Purpose or Unbleached Flour
   1 teaspoon vanilla
   ½ cup semi-sweet chocolate chips

FROSTING

   ¼ cup sugar
   ¼ cup firmly packed brown sugar
   ⅛ teaspoon salt
   ¼ cup milk
   2 tablespoons margarine or butter
   ½ cup semi-sweet chocolate chips
   1 cup powdered sugar, sifted
   ½ teaspoon vanilla

Heat oven to 350°F. Grease and flour bottom only of 13x9-inch pan. Dissolve instant coffee in hot water; set aside. In small saucepan over low heat, melt 1 cup chocolate chips, stirring constantly until smooth; set aside. In small bowl, beat egg whites until stiff peaks form; set aside.

In large bowl, beat 1 cup sugar and ½ cup margarine until light and fluffy. Add almond paste; blend well. Lightly spoon flour into measuring cup; level off. Stir in flour, dissolved coffee, melted chocolate, egg yolks and 1 teaspoon vanilla; mix well. Fold in beaten egg whites. Gently fold in ½ cup chocolate chips. Spread into prepared pan. Bake at 350°F. for 25 to 35 minutes or until set. DO NOT OVERBAKE. Cool completely.

n small saucepan, combine ¼ cup
ugar, brown sugar, salt, milk,
tablespoons margarine and ½ cup
hocolate chips. Bring to a boil over
nedium heat, stirring constantly.
keduce heat; simmer 3 minutes.
kemove from heat. Stir in powdered
ugar and ½ teaspoon vanilla; beat
intil smooth. Frost cooled brownies.
:ut into bars. Store in refrigerator.
·6 bars.

IIGH ALTITUDE—Above 3500 Feet:
Io Change.

,UTRITION INFORMATION PER SERVING

ERVING SIZE: BAR		PERCENT U.S. RDA PER SERVING	
ALORIES	160	PROTEIN	2%
ROTEIN	2g	VITAMIN A	2%
ARBOHYDRATE	21g	VITAMIN C	*
AT	8g	THIAMINE	2%
HOLESTEROL	30mg	RIBOFLAVIN	2%
ODIUM	55mg	NIACIN	*
OTASSIUM	70mg	CALCIUM	2%
		IRON	4%

Contains less than 2% of the U.S. RDA of this nutrient.

*You will need two sizes of heart-
shaped cookie cutters for this recipe.
The tip below describes how to make a
beautiful long-stemmed cookie
bouquet for a unique gift.*

Chocolate Valentine Cookies

COOKIE

- 1 cup sugar
- 1 cup margarine or butter, softened
- ¼ cup milk
- 1 teaspoon vanilla
- 1 egg
- 2¾ cups Pillsbury's BEST® All Purpose or Unbleached Flour
- ½ cup unsweetened cocoa
- ¾ teaspoon baking powder
- ¼ teaspoon baking soda

FROSTING

- 2 cups powdered sugar
- ½ cup margarine or butter, softened
- 2 to 3 tablespoons maraschino cherry juice or milk
  Red food color
  Powdered sugar, if desired

In large bowl, beat sugar and 1 cup
margarine until light and fluffy. Add
milk, vanilla and egg; blend well.
Lightly spoon flour into measuring
cup; level off. Stir in flour, cocoa,
baking powder and soda. Chill dough
1 hour for easier handling.

Heat oven to 350°F. On floured
surface, roll out dough, ⅓ at a time, to
⅛-inch thickness. Cut with floured
2½-inch heart-shaped cookie cutter.
Place half of the cutout hearts 1-inch
apart on ungreased cookie sheets. Cut
a 1-inch heart-shape from the centers
of remaining hearts. Place cutout
hearts on cookie sheets. Chill excess
dough and reroll. Bake at 350°F. for
9 to 11 minutes or until set.
Immediately remove from cookie
sheets; cool.

In small bowl, beat frosting
ingredients adding 1 tablespoon
cherry juice at a time for desired
spreading consistency. Tint with red
food color. Frost bottom side of whole
cookie. Top with cutout cookie. Dust
with powdered sugar.
4 dozen sandwich cookies.

TIP: To make a Valentine Heart Bouquet,
prepare cookies as directed above. Press
about 1½ inches of a 12-inch wooden
skewer into the frosting on the bottom
cookie. If necessary, spread additional
frosting to cover skewer. Top with cutout
cookie. Chill on cookie sheets for about
1 hour to set frosting. If desired, messages
or designs can be added with decorator
icing. Arrange bouquet in vase; add ribbon
bows, baby's breath, etc. as desired.

HIGH ALTITUDE—Above 3500 Feet: Decrease
baking powder to ¼ teaspoon. Bake as directed
above.

NUTRITION INFORMATION PER SERVING

SERVING SIZE: 1 COOKIE		PERCENT U.S. RDA PER SERVING	
CALORIES	120	PROTEIN	*
PROTEIN	1g	VITAMIN A	4%
CARBOHYDRATE	15g	VITAMIN C	*
FAT	6g	THIAMINE	2%
CHOLESTEROL	6mg	RIBOFLAVIN	2%
SODIUM	85mg	NIACIN	2%
POTASSIUM	25mg	CALCIUM	2%
		IRON	2%

*Contains less than 2% of the U.S. RDA of this nutrient.

Chocolate Valentine Cookies p. 31

This recipe is unbelievably easy to make with a saucepan method and unbelievably irresistible to eat.

Praline Caramel Divine Brownies

CRUST

  ¾ cup Pillsbury's BEST® All
      Purpose or Unbleached Flour
  ½ cup firmly packed brown sugar
  ¼ cup butter or margarine, melted
  ¾ cup finely chopped pecans

BROWNIE

  3 oz. (3 squares) unsweetened
      chocolate, chopped
  ¾ cup butter or margarine
  1½ teaspoons vanilla
  3 eggs
  ¾ cup sugar
  ½ cup firmly packed brown sugar
  1¼ cups Pillsbury's BEST® All
      Purpose or Unbleached Flour
  ¾ cup chopped pecans

FILLING

  1 can Pillsbury Ready To Spread
      Caramel Pecan Frosting
      Supreme

TOPPING

  1 oz. (1 square) unsweetened
      chocolate, chopped
  ¼ cup butter or margarine
  ¼ cup milk
  2¼ cups powdered sugar
  1 tablespoon vanilla

Heat oven to 350°F. Grease 13x9-inch pan. Lightly spoon flour into measuring cup; level off. In small bowl, combine crust ingredients. Press evenly into bottom of prepared pan.

In medium saucepan over low heat, melt 3 oz. chocolate and ¾ cup butter, stirring constantly until smooth. Remove from heat. Add 1½ teaspoons vanilla, eggs, sugar and ½ cup brown sugar; blend well. Stir in 1¼ cups flour and ¾ cup pecans; mix well. Spread over crust. Bake at 350°F. for 22 to 32 minutes or until set. Cool.

Spread filling over cooled brownies. In small saucepan over low heat, combine 1 oz. chocolate, ¼ cup butter and milk, stirring constantly until smooth. Remove from heat; stir in powdered sugar and vanilla until

smooth. Pour over filling; spread to cover. Refrigerate for 30 minutes. Cut into bars. Store in refrigerator. 48 bars

HIGH ALTITUDE—Above 3500 Feet:
No change.

If you are a frequent cookie baker, you may want to purchase a No. 40 ice cream scoop to use for dropping dough on cookie sheets. Cookies will be uniform in size and it takes about half the time to get a cookie sheet of dough ready for the oven.

Coconut Chocolate Chunk Cookies

COOKIE

  ¾ cup firmly packed brown
      sugar
  ½ cup sugar
  1 cup butter or margarine,
      softened
  2 eggs
  2 cups Pillsbury's BEST® All
      Purpose or Unbleached
      Flour
  ¼ cup unsweetened cocoa
  1 teaspoon baking soda
  ½ teaspoon salt
  5 oz. (5 squares) semi-sweet
      chocolate, chopped
  1 cup honey-roasted peanuts,
      coarsely chopped
  2 cups coconut

GLAZE

  1 cup powdered sugar
  1 to 2 tablespoons water

Heat oven to 350°F. In large bowl, beat brown sugar, sugar and butter until light and fluffy. Add eggs; blend well. Lightly spoon flour into measuring cup; level off. Stir in flour, cocoa, baking soda and salt; mix well. Add chocolate, peanuts and coconut.

Drop dough by ¼ cup measurement inches apart onto ungreased cookie heets. Bake at 350°F. for 13 to 5 minutes or until set. Cool 1 minute; emove from cookie sheets. Cool completely.

n small bowl, blend glaze ingredients, dding 1 tablespoon of water at a time or desired consistency. Drizzle over ookies. 2 dozen cookies.

HIGH ALTITUDE—Above 3500 Feet: Decrease aking soda to ¾ teaspoon. Bake as directed bove.

NUTRITION INFORMATION PER SERVING

SERVING SIZE: COOKIE		PERCENT U.S. RDA PER SERVING	
CALORIES	270	PROTEIN	6%
PROTEIN	4g	VITAMIN A	6%
CARBOHYDRATE	30g	VITAMIN C	*
FAT	15g	THIAMINE	6%
CHOLESTEROL	45mg	RIBOFLAVIN	2%
SODIUM	200 mg	NIACIN	6%
POTASSIUM	135mg	CALCIUM	4%
		IRON	6%

Contains less than 2% of the U.S. RDA of this nutrient.

White chocolate is a misnomer. It is not considered chocolate in the U.S. by the FDA because it does not contain "chocolate liquor" from the cocoa bean. Imported brands often include cocoa butter and additional flavorings. In this crunchy cookie, vanilla-flavored candy coating or vanilla-milk chips perform equally well.

White Chocolate Macadamia Nut Cookies

¾ cup firmly packed brown
    sugar
½ cup sugar
½ cup margarine or butter,
    softened
½ cup shortening
2 teaspoons vanilla
1 egg
1¾ cups Pillsbury's BEST® All
    Purpose or Unbleached
    Flour
1 teaspoon baking soda
½ teaspoon salt
8 oz. vanilla-flavored candy
    coating, coarsely chopped
    or 1⅓ cups vanilla-milk
    chips
3½-oz. jar macadamia nuts, coarsely
    chopped

Heat oven to 375°F. In large bowl, beat brown sugar, sugar, margarine and shortening until light and fluffy. Add vanilla and egg; blend well. Lightly spoon flour into measuring cup; level off. Stir in flour, baking soda and salt; mix well. Stir in candy coating and macadamia nuts. Drop dough by tablespoonfuls 3 inches apart onto ungreased cookie sheets. Bake at 375°F. for 8 to 10 minutes or until light golden brown. Cool 1 minute; remove from cookie sheets. 4 dozen cookies.

HIGH ALTITUDE—Above 3500 Feet: Decrease baking soda to ¾ teaspoon. Decrease margarine to 6 tablespoons. Bake as directed above.

NUTRITION INFORMATION PER SERVING

SERVING SIZE: 1 COOKIE		PERCENT U.S. RDA PER SERVING	
CALORIES	110	PROTEIN	*
PROTEIN	1g	VITAMIN A	*
CARBOHYDRATE	12g	VITAMIN C	*
FAT	7g	THIAMINE	2%
CHOLESTEROL	6mg	RIBOFLAVIN	*
SODIUM	70mg	NIACIN	*
POTASSIUM	45mg	CALCIUM	*
		IRON	2%

*Contains less than 2% of the U.S. RDA of this nutrient.

COOK'S NOTE

What is an easy method to grease and flour pans?
If you do a lot of baking, try this easy method for greasing and flouring pans. In small bowl, blend 1 cup shortening and 1 cup all purpose flour until well mixed. Store in air-tight container. To grease pan, use pastry brush dipped in shortening-flour mixture.

Pictured top to bottom: Peanut Butter Chocolate Squares, Double Chocolate Cookies

Ever heard of a reverse chocolate chip cookie? In this recipe, the chocolate color in the dough is from cocoa and vanilla-milk chips replace chocolate chips. A great milk-dunking cookie.

Double Chocolate Cookies

~~~~~~

¾ cup firmly packed brown sugar
½ cup sugar
¾ cup margarine or butter,
    softened
¼ cup shortening
1½ teaspoons vanilla
  1 egg
1¾ cups Pillsbury's BEST® All
    Purpose or Unbleached Flour
¼ cup unsweetened cocoa
  1 teaspoon baking soda
½ teaspoon salt
  1 cup vanilla-milk chips
½ cup chopped nuts, if desired

Heat oven to 375°F. In large bowl, beat brown sugar, sugar, margarine and shortening until light and fluffy. Add vanilla and egg; beat well. Lightly spoon flour into measuring cup; level off. Add flour, cocoa, baking soda and salt; mix well. Stir in vanilla chips and nuts. Drop dough by teaspoonful 2 inches apart onto ungreased cookie sheets. Bake at 375°F. for 7 to 10 minutes or until set. Cool 1 minute; remove from cookie sheets.
3 dozen cookies.

HIGH ALTITUDE—Above 3500 Feet: Decrease baking soda to ¾ teaspoon. Decrease margarine to ½ cup. Bake as directed above.

NUTRITION INFORMATION PER SERVING

SERVING SIZE: 1 COOKIE		PERCENT U.S. RDA PER SERVING	
CALORIES	140	PROTEIN	2%
PROTEIN	1g	VITAMIN A	2%
CARBOHYDRATE	15g	VITAMIN C	*
FAT	8g	THIAMINE	2%
CHOLESTEROL	8mg	RIBOFLAVIN	*
SODIUM	115mg	NIACIN	*
POTASSIUM	55mg	CALCIUM	2%
		IRON	4%

*Contains less than 2% of the U.S. RDA of this nutrient.

Two favorite flavor combinations— peanut butter and chocolate—are outstanding in this simple, make-in-a-hurry recipe.

Peanut Butter Chocolate Squares

~~~~~~

SQUARE
½ cup firmly packed brown sugar
½ cup sugar
  1 cup margarine or butter,
    softened
  2 eggs
  1 cup Pillsbury's BEST® All
    Purpose or Unbleached
    Flour
  1 cup rolled oats
  1 cup peanut butter chips
TOPPING
6-oz. pkg. (1 cup) semi-sweet
    chocolate chips
  3 tablespoons margarine or
    butter
½ cup chopped peanuts

Heat oven to 350°F. Grease 13x9-inch pan. In large bowl, beat brown sugar, sugar and 1 cup margarine until light and fluffy. Add eggs; blend well. Lightly spoon flour into measuring cup; level off. Add flour, oats and peanut butter chips; mix well. Spread into prepared pan. Bake at 350°F. for 20 to 30 minutes or until light golden brown around edges. Cool slightly.

In small saucepan over low heat, melt chocolate chips and 3 tablespoons margarine, stirring constantly. Spread over squares; sprinkle with peanuts. Cut into squares. 36 squares.

HIGH ALTITUDE—Above 3500 Feet: No change.

NUTRITION INFORMATION PER SERVING

SERVING SIZE: 1 SQUARE		PERCENT U.S. RDA PER SERVING	
CALORIES	180	PROTEIN	4%
PROTEIN	3g	VITAMIN A	8%
CARBOHYDRATE	15g	VITAMIN C	*
FAT	12g	THIAMINE	4%
CHOLESTEROL	15mg	RIBOFLAVIN	2%
SODIUM	125mg	NIACIN	8%
POTASSIUM	95mg	CALCIUM	2%
		IRON	6%

*Contains less than 2% of the U.S. RDA of this nutrient.

Designer Desserts

Designer Desserts

Deluxe, delectable and designed to WOW!

G o for it! The ultimate in extraordinary finales to bring chocolate lovers' richest fantasies to life. Airy souffles, tantalizing tortes, silky flans, delicate mousses and meringues and other gourmet show-stoppers will remind you of the very best desserts you have ever tasted—anywhere.

Rest assured. **Every** recipe here, even those with some intricate-appearing steps, is in reach of most cooks. Preparation techniques are really quite basic—whisking, folding, cooking a custard, unmolding and creating eye-catching garnishes. Each and every procedure is described in detail to guide you from start to glorious finish with confidence. We think you will be amazed at the impressive results, especially if you consider yourself a beginning or "rusty" cook.

With February just days away, we have included some sweet stunners for celebrating in style this month of hearts and flowers and presidential birthdays. Fruit-Filled Chocolate Meringues, Chocolate Heart and Cookies 'n Cream Wedges are memorable enough for any holiday or special occasion. Liqueur-laced cremes, sauces and fillings, rich toppings and glazes and other touches dress these desserts to dazzle!

make this recipe low-calorie, skip
e fudge sauce. It's just as wonderful.

Fruit-Filled
Chocolate Meringues

ERINGUES
   2 egg whites
   ¼ teaspoon salt
   ¼ teaspoon vinegar
   ½ cup sugar
   ½ teaspoon vanilla
   1 tablespoon unsweetened
       cocoa

LLING
to 1½ cups assorted fresh fruits,
       such as sliced peaches,
       strawberries, blueberries,
       grapes, kiwifruit or
       raspberries
   Fudge sauce, if desired

eat oven to 275°F. Line cookie sheet
ith parchment paper. In small bowl,
eat egg whites, salt and vinegar until
amy. Gradually add sugar and
anilla, beating until stiff peaks form.
ft cocoa over beaten egg whites and
ld into mixture.

sing a heaping tablespoonful of egg
hite mixture, drop 6 individual
ounds of mixture onto parchment-
ned cookie sheet. Make a deep well
the center of each, spreading egg
hite mixture to form a 3-inch circle.
ake at 275°F. for 45 minutes or until
isp. Turn off oven; keep door closed
r 1½ hours. Remove meringues from
ven. Cool completely. Remove from
archment paper.

efore serving, fill meringues with
esh fruit and serve with fudge sauce,
desired. 6 servings.

JTRITION INFORMATION PER SERVING

RVING SIZE: OF RECIPE		PERCENT U.S. RDA PER SERVING	
LORIES	150	PROTEIN	2%
OTEIN	2g	VITAMIN A	4%
RBOHYDRATE	35g	VITAMIN C	4%
	0g	THIAMINE	*
OLESTEROL	0mg	RIBOFLAVIN	4%
DIUM	135mg	NIACIN	2%
TASSIUM	130mg	CALCIUM	*
		IRON	*

ontains less than 2% of the U.S. RDA of this nutrient.

COOK'S NOTE

What do I need to know about meringues?

♥ A meringue consists chiefly of
three ingredients: egg whites
(for volume), sugar (for
sweetness) and cream of
tartar (a stabilizer).

♥ It is essential to use grease-
free utensils and equipment.
A small amount of fat can
reduce the volume of the
whipped egg whites.

♥ It's best to avoid making
meringues on hot, humid
days. They may not have the
volume they would normally
have and may weep after
baking.

A cold, creamy dessert.

Chilled Kahlua Souffle

2 envelopes unflavored gelatin
2 cups cold milk
1/2 cup unsweetened cocoa
6 tablespoons sugar
2 tablespoons firmly packed brown sugar
1/4 cup coffee-flavored liqueur
3 eggs, separated
1 cup whipping cream
  Whipped cream
  Grated Chocolate (see Index)

In small bowl, combine gelatin and milk; let stand 5 minutes to soften. In medium saucepan over low heat, combine gelatin mixture, cocoa, 2 tablespoons of the sugar, brown sugar, liqueur and 3 egg yolks; stir constantly until gelatin is dissolved and mixture coats the back of a spoon. DO NOT BOIL. Remove from heat; transfer to a large bowl. Refrigerate mixture just until slightly thickened, about 1 hour.

In small bowl, beat whipping cream until stiff peaks form. In small bowl, beat egg whites until soft peaks form. Gradually add remaining 4 tablespoons sugar and beat until stiff peaks form. Fold into chocolate mixture. Spoon into 1-quart souffle dish. Refrigerate at least 6 hours or overnight. Garnish with whipped cream and Grated Chocolate. 8 servings.

NUTRITION INFORMATION PER SERVING

SERVING SIZE: 1/18 OF RECIPE		PERCENT U.S. RDA PER SERVING	
CALORIES	311	PROTEIN	10%
PROTEIN	8g	VITAMIN A	15%
CARBOHYDRATE	27g	VITAMIN C	*
FAT	19g	THIAMINE	2%
CHOLESTEROL	160mg	RIBOFLAVIN	10%
SODIUM	110mg	NIACIN	*
POTASSIUM	200mg	CALCIUM	10%
		IRON	6%

*Contains less than 2% of the U.S. RDA of this nutrient.

This light delicacy will melt in your mouth. This recipe requires careful attention while preparing, but it's worth every bite.

Chocolate Cream Mousse

6-oz. pkg. (1 cup) semi-sweet chocolate chips
5 eggs, separated
2 tablespoons milk
3 tablespoons chocolate-flavored liqueur
2 cups whipping cream
5 tablespoons sugar
  Whipping cream, whipped, sweetened
  Frozen boysenberries, thawed and drained, or any favorite fruit
  Chocolate Leaves, if desired (see Index)

In small saucepan over low heat, melt chocolate chips, stirring constantly until smooth. Remove from heat; cool

In small saucepan over very low heat, combine 5 egg yolks and milk. Whisk vigorously and constantly until the yolks begin to thicken. Add the liqueur and continue whisking just until the mixture thickens and heavily coats the back of a spoon; remove from heat. Whisk in melted chocolate; transfer to large bowl.

In large bowl, beat whipping cream and 2 tablespoons sugar until stiff peaks form. Fold into chocolate mixture.

In medium bowl, beat egg whites until soft peaks form. Gradually add 3 tablespoons sugar and beat until stiff peaks form. Fold into chocolate mixture. Store in refrigerator.

Spoon mixture into pastry bag with desired decorating tip; pipe mousse into sherbet glasses or dessert dishes. Garnish as desired with whipped cream, boysenberries and Chocolate Leaves. 8 (1-cup) servings.

NUTRITION INFORMATION PER SERVING

SERVING SIZE: CUP		PERCENT U.S. RDA PER SERVING	
CALORIES	490	PROTEIN	10%
PROTEIN	7g	VITAMIN A	25%
CARBOHYDRATE	31g	VITAMIN C	*
FAT	38g	THIAMINE	2%
CHOLESTEROL	260mg	RIBOFLAVIN	10%
SODIUM	70mg	NIACIN	*
POTASSIUM	200mg	CALCIUM	8%
		IRON	8%

*Contains less than 2% of the U.S. RDA of this nutrient.

Recipes requiring cocoa refer to the unsweetened type, not instant cocoa mix or other combinations containing sweeteners. Measure lump-free as you do flour and sugar.

Light Chocolate Pudding

½ cup sugar
⅓ cup unsweetened cocoa
2 tablespoons cornstarch
2½ cups low-fat milk
2 eggs, slightly beaten
1 tablespoon vanilla
   Fresh fruit, if desired

In medium heavy saucepan, combine sugar, cocoa and cornstarch; mix well. Gradually stir in milk and eggs. Cook over medium heat until mixture comes to a boil, stirring constantly; boil 1 minute. Remove from heat; stir in vanilla. Cool slightly; pour into serving dishes. Garnish with fresh fruit. Store any remaining pudding in refrigerator. 6 (½-cup) servings.

■ MICROWAVE DIRECTIONS: In medium microwave-safe bowl, combine sugar, cocoa and cornstarch; mix well. Add milk and eggs; blend well. Microwave on HIGH 7 to 8 minutes or until pudding is thickened, stirring every 2 minutes. Blend in vanilla; stir until smooth.

NUTRITION INFORMATION PER SERVING

SERVING SIZE: 1/2 CUP		PERCENT U.S. RDA PER SERVING	
CALORIES	180	PROTEIN	10%
PROTEIN	6g	VITAMIN A	6%
CARBOHYDRATE	27g	VITAMIN C	15%
FAT	5g	THIAMINE	4%
CHOLESTEROL	100mg	RIBOFLAVIN	15%
SODIUM	110mg	NIACIN	*
POTASSIUM	240mg	CALCIUM	15%
		IRON	4%

*Contains less than 2% of the U.S. RDA of this nutrient.

A rich, full-flavored pudding that is especially easy to make in the microwave oven.

Classic Chocolate Pudding

¾ cup sugar
2 tablespoons cornstarch
⅛ teaspoon salt
2 cups milk
2 oz. (2 squares) unsweetened chocolate, chopped
1 egg, slightly beaten
1 tablespoon margarine or butter, softened
1 teaspoon vanilla
   Whipped cream

In medium heavy saucepan, combine sugar, cornstarch and salt; mix well. Gradually stir in milk and chocolate. Cook over medium heat until mixture comes to a boil, stirring constantly; boil 1 minute. Blend small amount of hot mixture with egg; add egg mixture to remaining hot mixture. Cook over medium heat just until mixture comes to a boil. Remove from heat; stir in margarine and vanilla. Cool slightly; spoon into serving dishes. Garnish with whipped cream. Store in refrigerator. 5 (½-cup) servings.

■ MICROWAVE DIRECTIONS: In medium microwave-safe bowl, combine sugar, cornstarch and salt; mix well. Add milk and egg; blend well. Add chocolate. Microwave on HIGH for 7 to 8 minutes or until pudding is thickened, stirring every 2 minutes. Blend in margarine and vanilla; stir until smooth.

NUTRITION INFORMATION PER SERVING

SERVING SIZE: 1/2 CUP		PERCENT U.S. RDA PER SERVING	
CALORIES	310	PROTEIN	8%
PROTEIN	6g	VITAMIN A	8%
CARBOHYDRATE	41g	VITAMIN C	*
FAT	14g	THIAMINE	2%
CHOLESTEROL	80mg	RIBOFLAVIN	10%
SODIUM	140mg	NIACIN	*
POTASSIUM	270mg	CALCIUM	15%
		IRON	6%

*Contains less than 2% of the U.S. RDA of this nutrient.

A chocolate lover's fantasy in flavor and very attractive to serve.

Creamy Chocolate Lace Cheesecake

CRUST

1½ cups chocolate wafer crumbs
½ cup finely chopped almonds
¼ cup margarine or butter, melted

FILLING

2 (8-oz.) pkg. cream cheese, softened
⅔ cup sugar
3 eggs
12-oz. pkg. (2 cups) semi-sweet chocolate chips, melted, cooled
1 cup whipping cream
2 tablespoons margarine or butter, melted
1 teaspoon vanilla

TOPPING

1 cup dairy sour cream
1½ teaspoons vanilla
1 teaspoon sugar
½ oz. (½ square) unsweetened chocolate, melted

Heat oven to 325°F. Butter 9-inch springform pan. In large bowl, blend crust ingredients. Press into bottom and up sides of prepared pan; refrigerate. In large bowl, beat cream cheese and ⅔ cup sugar until smooth. Add eggs, one at a time, beating well after each addition. Add melted chocolate chips; beat well. Add whipping cream, 2 tablespoons margarine and 1 teaspoon vanilla; beat until smooth. Pour into prepared crust. Bake at 325°F. for 55 to 65 minutes or until edges are set. Center of cheese cake will be soft. (To minimize cracking, place shallow pan half full of water on lower oven rack during baking.) Cool in pan 5 minutes. carefully remove sides of pan Cool completely.

In small bowl, combine sour cream, 1½ teaspoons vanilla and 1 teaspoon sugar; stir until smooth. Spread over cooled cheesecake. Drizzle with ½ oz melted chocolate in lace pattern. Refrigerate several hours or overnigh before serving. Garnish as desired. 16 servings.

NUTRITION INFORMATION PER SERVING

SERVING SIZE: 1/16 OF RECIPE		PERCENT U.S. RDA PER SERVING	
CALORIES	470	PROTEIN	10%
PROTEIN	7g	VITAMIN A	20%
CARBOHYDRATE	31g	VITAMIN C	*
FAT	36g	THIAMINE	4%
CHOLESTEROL	110mg	RIBOFLAVIN	10%
SODIUM	180mg	NIACIN	2%
POTASSIUM	200mg	CALCIUM	8%
		IRON	8%

*Contains less than 2% of the U.S. RDA of this nutrient.

COOK'S NOTE

What causes chocolate to thicken or "seize" when melting?

When chocolate has "seized", it could be one or a combination of the following factors:

♥ *Heat that is too high (above 120°F.)*
♥ *Condensation of steam droplets*
♥ *Water drops on utensils or equipment*

All is not lost! To return chocolate to its original consistency, stir in 1 teaspoon solid shortening (not butter since it contains water) for every 2 ounces of chocolate used.

Creamy Chocolate Lace Cheesecake

Every bite of this heavenly dessert melts in your mouth.

Layered Chocolate Frozen Mousse Torte

CRUST
1½ cups finely chopped macadamia
    nuts
2 tablespoons powdered sugar
¼ cup butter, melted

FILLING
4 oz. white chocolate, chopped
4 tablespoons butter
4 oz. (4 squares) semi-sweet
    chocolate, chopped
6 eggs, separated
½ cup milk
1 cup powdered sugar
⅛ teaspoon cream of tartar
1 cup whipping cream, whipped
2 teaspoons grated orange peel

GARNISH
1 large orange
¼ cup water
¼ cup powdered sugar
½ oz. (½ square) semi-sweet
    chocolate, melted

Heat oven to 350°F. In small bowl, combine crust ingredients; mix well. Press firmly into bottom of 9-inch springform pan. Bake at 350°F. for 10 minutes; cool.

In small saucepan over low heat, melt white chocolate and 2 tablespoons of the butter, stirring constantly until smooth; set aside. In another small saucepan over low heat, melt semi-sweet chocolate and 2 tablespoons remaining butter, stirring constantly until smooth; set aside.

In medium heavy saucepan over low heat, combine egg yolks, milk and 1 cup powdered sugar, whisking constantly until mixture thickens, about 5 minutes. Pour half of egg yolk mixture into each bowl of chocolate. Stir until smooth.

In large bowl, beat 6 egg whites with cream of tartar until stiff peaks form. Fold half of beaten egg whites, whipped cream and grated orange peel into each chocolate mixture. Spoon dark chocolate mixture over

crust. Freeze 5 minutes. Spoon white chocolate mixture over dark chocolate layer. Freeze 8 hours or overnight.

Remove peel from orange. Cut peel into ⅛ to ¼-inch thin strips. In small saucepan over medium heat, boil peel, water and powdered sugar about 15 minutes or until peel is tender.

Remove from heat; drain. Dry peels on paper towels. Place on waxed paper-covered cookie sheets; drizzle with melted chocolate. Refrigerate 10 minutes to set. Remove sides of pan; let torte stand at room temperature 15 minutes before serving. Garnish with candied orange peel. Store any remaining torte in freezer. 16 servings.

NUTRITION INFORMATION PER SERVING

SERVING SIZE: 1/16 OF RECIPE		PERCENT U.S. RDA PER SERVING	
CALORIES	340	PROTEIN	6%
PROTEIN	4g	VITAMIN A	10%
CARBOHYDRATE	20g	VITAMIN C	2%
FAT	27g	THIAMINE	4%
CHOLESTEROL	140mg	RIBOFLAVIN	6%
SODIUM	95mg	NIACIN	*
POTASSIUM	140mg	CALCIUM	4%
		IRON	6%

*Contains less than 2% of the U.S. RDA of this nutrient.

For an elegant, impressive presentation, serve the Creme Anglaise in the center of the souffle. A well forms naturally as the souffle begins to fall after it is removed from the oven.

Baked Chocolate Souffle with Brandy Creme Anglaise

CREME ANGLAISE
2 egg yolks
¼ cup sugar
1 cup whipping cream
1½ teaspoons brandy

SOUFFLE
6 eggs, separated
½ cup sugar
¼ teaspoon salt
4 oz. (4 squares) semi-sweet
    chocolate, chopped
¼ teaspoon cream of tartar
    Powdered sugar

small bowl, combine 2 egg yolks
d ¼ cup sugar. In small saucepan
er low heat, bring whipping cream
st to a boil. Blend a small amount of
t whipping cream into yolks. Blend
g yolk mixture into whipping cream
d cook over low heat about
minutes or until custard coats a
oon, stirring constantly. DO NOT
IL. Remove from heat. Stir in
andy. Cover surface with waxed
per. Cool slightly; refrigerate.

at oven to 375°F. Butter 1½-quart
uffle dish. Fold a 25-inch piece of
l lengthwise into thirds. Butter one
le of foil; position foil, buttered side
around the outside of prepared
uffle dish, allowing foil to extend
nches above rim of dish; secure
ds with tape.

large bowl, beat 6 egg yolks, ½ cup
gar and salt about 5 minutes or until
ick and lemon-colored. In small
ucepan over low heat, melt
ocolate, stirring constantly until
nooth. Stir melted chocolate into egg
lk mixture until well combined. In
all bowl, beat egg whites and cream
tartar until stiff peaks form.
adually fold beaten egg whites into
ocolate mixture. Spoon gently into
epared souffle dish. Bake at 375°F.
r 45 minutes. Dust with powdered
gar after baking; serve immediately.
serve, pour about 2 tablespoons
eme Anglaise onto plate, spoon
uffle on top. Refrigerate any
maining dessert. 12 servings.

TRITION INFORMATION PER SERVING

VING SIZE: 2 OF RECIPE		PERCENT U.S. RDA PER SERVING	
ORIES	220	PROTEIN	6%
TEIN	4g	VITAMIN A	10%
RBOHYDRATE	19g	VITAMIN C	*
	14g	THIAMINE	2%
LESTEROL	210mg	RIBOFLAVIN	6%
IUM	85mg	NIACIN	*
ASSIUM	80mg	CALCIUM	2%
		IRON	4%

ntains less than 2% of the U.S. RDA of this nutrient.

The caramel runs down the sides of the custard forming a sauce when the flan is unmolded. It's wonderful warm or cold.

Caramel-Topped Chocolate Flan

CARAMEL
⅓ cup sugar
2 tablespoons water
⅛ teaspoon cream of tartar

FLAN
1⅓ cups half-and-half
3 oz. (¾ bar) sweet cooking
   chocolate, chopped
2 tablespoons sugar
3 eggs
½ teaspoon vanilla

In small heavy saucepan over medium heat, combine all caramel ingredients until mixture comes to a boil, stirring constantly. Let boil without stirring until mixture begins to caramelize, about 10 to 12 minutes. If it darkens in one spot, swirl pan around gently. Stir until mixture is a medium caramel color. Immediately pour caramel into the bottom of six 6-oz. custard cups; set aside.

In small saucepan over low heat, combine half-and-half, chocolate and 2 tablespoons sugar, stirring constantly until smooth. Remove from heat. In small bowl, beat eggs and vanilla until light and lemon-colored. Gradually add chocolate mixture; blend well. Carefully pour custard over caramel in custard cups. Place cups in 13x9-inch pan. Pour very hot water into pan within ½ inch of tops of custard cups. Bake at 325°F. for 50 minutes or until knife inserted in center comes out clean. Unmold and serve warm or refrigerate in custard cups and serve cold. Garnish with whipped cream and fresh fruit, if desired. Refrigerate any remaining flan. 6 servings.

NUTRITION INFORMATION PER SERVING

SERVING SIZE: 1/6 OF RECIPE		PERCENT U.S. RDA PER SERVING	
CALORIES	300	PROTEIN	8%
PROTEIN	6g	VITAMIN A	15%
CARBOHYDRATE	31g	VITAMIN C	6%
FAT	17g	THIAMINE	2%
CHOLESTEROL	170mg	RIBOFLAVIN	10%
SODIUM	65mg	NIACIN	2%
POTASSIUM	230mg	CALCIUM	8%
		IRON	4%

The filling in the recipe has a light texture from folding in whipped cream. A sensational no-bake recipe everyone will love.

Cookies 'n Cream Wedges

CRUST

> 2 cups finely crushed creme-filled chocolate sandwich cookies (about 24 cookies)
> ⅓ cup margarine or butter, melted

FILLING

2 (8-oz.) pkg. cream cheese, softened
> ⅔ cup sugar
> 1 tablespoon vanilla
> 1 cup whipping cream, whipped
> 2 oz. (2 squares) semi-sweet chocolate, grated
> Chocolate Cut-Outs (see Index)

In large bowl, combine crust ingredients. Press into bottom and up sides of 9-inch springform pan; refrigerate.

In large bowl, beat cream cheese until light and fluffy. Gradually add sugar and vanilla; blend well. Fold in whipped cream and grated chocolate. Spoon into crust. Refrigerate at least 2 hours before serving. With small sharp knife, loosen crust around rim of pan. Remove sides of pan; cut into wedges. Garnish with Chocolate Cut-Outs or as desired. Refrigerate any remaining dessert. 16 servings.

NUTRITION INFORMATION PER SERVING

SERVING SIZE: 1/16 OF RECIPE		PERCENT U.S. RDA PER SERVING	
CALORIES	300	PROTEIN	4%
PROTEIN	3g	VITAMIN A	15%
CARBOHYDRATE	21g	VITAMIN C	*
FAT	23g	THIAMINE	2%
CHOLESTEROL	60mg	RIBOFLAVIN	6%
SODIUM	200mg	NIACIN	*
POTASSIUM	65mg	CALCIUM	4%
		IRON	4%

*Contains less than 2% of the U.S. RDA of this nutrient.

The perfect make-ahead, no-bake dessert for bridge club.

Raspberry Dessert Squares

CRUST
- 8½-oz. pkg. chocolate cookie wafers, crushed, reserving 2 teaspoons for garnish
- ½ cup butter or margarine, melted

FILLING
- 2 (10-oz.) pkg. frozen raspberries, drained, reserving liquid
- 2 tablespoons cornstarch
- 2 cups powdered sugar
- 2 tablespoons unsweetened cocoa
- ¾ cup butter or margarine, softened

TOPPING
- 1½ cups whipping cream, whipped, sweetened
- Reserved 2 teaspoons crushed chocolate cookie wafers

Butter 13x9-inch pan. In small bowl, combine wafers and melted butter. Press into bottom of prepared pan.

In small saucepan, combine reserved raspberry liquid and cornstarch. Bring to a boil over medium heat, stirring constantly until thickened; cool. Fold in raspberries.

In small bowl, beat powdered sugar, cocoa and ¾ cup butter until light and fluffy. Carefully spread mixture on crumb crust. Refrigerate until firm. Spoon raspberry mixture over butter layer. Spread with sweetened whipped cream and sprinkle with reserved crushed cookies. Store in refrigerator. 16 servings.

NUTRITION INFORMATION PER SERVING

SERVING SIZE: 1/16 OF RECIPE		PERCENT U.S. RDA PER SERVING	
CALORIES	360	PROTEIN	2%
PROTEIN	2g	VITAMIN A	20%
CARBOHYDRATE	32g	VITAMIN C	6%
FAT	25g	THIAMINE	2%
CHOLESTEROL	70mg	RIBOFLAVIN	4%
SODIUM	180mg	NIACIN	2%
POTASSIUM	80mg	CALCIUM	2%
		IRON	4%

An easy microwave recipe from a recent Bake-Off®

Chocolate Cherry Crunch

- 1½ cups Pillsbury's BEST® All Purpose or Unbleached Flour
- 1 cup firmly packed brown sugar
- ¾ cup quick-cooking rolled oats
- ¼ cup unsweetened cocoa
- ½ teaspoon baking soda
- ¼ teaspoon salt
- ½ cup margarine or butter, softened
- 21-oz. can cherry fruit pie filling
- 1 teaspoon brandy extract, if desired

■ MICROWAVE DIRECTIONS:
Lightly spoon flour into measuring cup; level off. In large bowl, combine flour, brown sugar, oats, cocoa, baking soda and salt; cut in margarine until mixture is crumbly and well blended. Press 1 cup crumb mixture into bottom of 8 or 9-inch square microwave-safe dish. Combine pie filling and brandy extract; spoon evenly over crust. Sprinkle remaining crumb mixture evenly over cherry filling; press lightly over filling.

Microwave on HIGH for 13 to 15 minutes or until firm and cracks appear in topping. Cool on flat surface. Serve with ice cream or whipped cream, if desired. 6 to 8 servings.

HIGH ALTITUDE—Above 3500 Feet: No change.

NUTRITION INFORMATION PER SERVING

SERVING SIZE: 1/8 OF RECIPE		PERCENT U.S. RDA PER SERVING	
CALORIES	460	PROTEIN	6%
PROTEIN	4g	VITAMIN A	15%
CARBOHYDRATE	82g	VITAMIN C	2%
FAT	13g	THIAMINE	15%
CHOLESTEROL	0mg	RIBOFLAVIN	6%
SODIUM	330mg	NIACIN	8%
POTASSIUM	220mg	CALCIUM	8%
		IRON	15%

*Make this special recipe for your
sweetheart in a heart-shaped mold for
Valentine's Day.*

Chocolate Heart

CHOCOLATE CREAM

 4 oz. (4 squares) semi-sweet
  chocolate, chopped
(8-oz.) pkg. cream cheese, softened
 2 cups whipping cream
 2 cups powdered sugar
 1 tablespoon cherry-flavored
  liqueur

SAUCE

 10-oz. pkg. frozen strawberries,
  thawed
 3 tablespoons powdered
  sugar
 1 tablespoon cherry-flavored
  liqueur
  Fresh strawberries, sliced
  White Chocolate Piping
  (see Index)

Line 8-cup heart-shaped or other
decorative mold with dampened
cheesecloth, two layers thick,
extending 2 inches beyond mold. In
small saucepan over low heat, melt
chocolate, stirring constantly until
smooth; cool. In large bowl, beat
cream cheese until light and fluffy.
Gradually add ½ cup of the whipping
cream; beat until smooth and creamy.
Blend in 2 cups powdered sugar, 1
tablespoon liqueur and cooled
chocolate; mix well. In small bowl,
beat remaining 1½ cups whipping
cream until soft peaks form. Fold
whipped cream into chocolate
mixture. Spoon into mold. Fold
extended cheesecloth over top of
chocolate mixture. Refrigerate
overnight.

Puree strawberries in blender
container or food processor. Strain
through fine sieve to remove seeds.
Stir in 3 tablespoons powdered sugar
and 1 tablespoon liqueur. To serve,
pull back cheesecloth and invert to
unmold on serving platter; remove
cheesecloth. Arrange sliced
strawberries on mold. Garnish with
White Chocolate Piping or as desired.
Serve with strawberry sauce.
Refrigerate any remaining dessert.
12 to 16 servings.

NUTRITION INFORMATION PER SERVING

SERVING SIZE: 1/16 OF RECIPE		PERCENT U.S. RDA PER SERVING	
CALORIES	330	PROTEIN	4%
PROTEIN	3g	VITAMIN A	15%
CARBOHYDRATE	26g	VITAMIN C	20%
FAT	24g	THIAMINE	*
CHOLESTEROL	70mg	RIBOFLAVIN	6%
SODIUM	95mg	NIACIN	*
POTASSIUM	110mg	CALCIUM	4%
		IRON	4%

*Contains less than 2% of the U.S. RDA of this nutrient.

French Butter Cream Chocolate Cake p. 58

Cakes & Pies

Cakes & Pies

When you're cooking for compliments.

Sugar and spice seldom look as nice as in a tender, tasty cake or pie. And when that delicacy features chocolate as a main ingredient, it soars to irresistible status.

Some of these cake recipes are sure to evoke fond memories. The rich Chocolate Date Cake and moist Cocoa Oatmeal Cake are reminiscent of family favorites and potluck specialties. We never tire of these hand-me-downs that seem to taste better with every baking. Or sample microwave recipes, each featuring creative touches to transform plain to fancy in just minutes. Definitely dressed for success are the Mocha Chocolate Cream Torte or luscious layered French Buttercream Chocolate Cake. Don't be deterred by the elegant names—explicit instructions make them as easy as they are exquisite.

All Ready Pie Crusts and delectable crumb crusts streamline the pie and tart collection. Crusts are made in minutes to hold a scrumptious selection of fillings from cream to chiffon, preserves to ice cream. And the delicious tortes will set the stage for a super special dessert or snack.

stunning, layered torte with the irresistible flavors of coffee and chocolate combined.

Mocha Chocolate Cream Torte

CRUST
- 1½ cups chopped hazelnuts
- ½ cup powdered sugar
- ¼ cup butter or margarine, melted

FUDGE LAYER
- 6 oz. pkg. (1 cup) semi-sweet chocolate chips
- 1 tablespoon instant coffee
- 1 cup whipping cream
- ¼ cup butter or margarine,

CHOCOLATE CREAM LAYER
- 1 cup powdered sugar
- 1 cup butter or margarine, softened
- ½ cup whipping cream
- 3 oz. (3 squares) semi-sweet chocolate, melted, cooled

TOPPING
- 1 tablespoon powdered sugar
- 1 teaspoon unsweetened cocoa
- ½ cup whipping cream, whipped
  Candied coffee beans or chocolate chips, if desired
  Chocolate Shavings, if desired
  (see Index)

Heat oven to 375°F. In small bowl, combine crust ingredients; mix well. Press firmly into bottom of 9-inch springform pan. Bake at 375°F. for 8 to 10 minutes or until light golden brown; cool.

In small saucepan over low heat, melt chocolate chips, instant coffee and whipping cream, stirring constantly until smooth. Remove from heat; stir in ¼ cup butter. Refrigerate until lightly thickened. Spread over crust; freeze until firm.

In medium bowl, cream 1 cup powdered sugar and 1 cup butter until light and fluffy. Add ½ cup whipping cream, beating at medium speed until smooth. Blend in melted chocolate. Spread over fudge layer. Refrigerate one hour.

In small bowl, fold 1 tablespoon powdered sugar and cocoa into whipped cream. Spoon topping into pastry bag with desired decorative tip;

pipe rosettes evenly spaced around top edge of torte. Garnish with candied coffee beans or chocolate chips or Chocolate Shavings. Store in refrigerator. 16 servings.

NUTRITION INFORMATION PER SERVING

SERVING SIZE: 1/16 OF RECIPE		PERCENT U.S. RDA PER SERVING	
CALORIES	450	PROTEIN	4%
PROTEIN	3g	VITAMIN A	20%
CARBOHYDRATE	25g	VITAMIN C	*
DIETARY FIBER	3g	THIAMINE	4%
FAT	40g	RIBOFLAVIN	4%
POLYUNSATURATED	2g	NIACIN	*
SATURATED	21g	CALCIUM	4%
CHOLESTEROL	87mg	IRON	4%
SODIUM	190mg		
POTASSIUM	150mg		

*Contains less than 2% of the U.S. RDA of this nutrient.

This is so good it could well become everyone's favorite.

Ice Cream Sundae Pie

CRUST
- 9-inch prepared chocolate wafer crust

FILLING
- 1 cup vanilla ice cream, softened
- ¼ cup caramel ice cream topping
- 1 cup chocolate ice cream, softened
- ¼ cup marshmallow creme
- ¼ cup fudge ice cream topping
- ½ cup coarsely chopped pecans
- 1 cup whipped topping
- 6 to 8 maraschino cherries with stems, drained

Spread vanilla ice cream evenly into prepared crust. Pour caramel topping evenly over vanilla ice cream. Spread chocolate ice cream over caramel topping. Drop marshmallow creme by teaspoonful over chocolate ice cream. Pour fudge topping over marshmallow creme. Sprinkle with pecans. Wrap tightly with foil; freeze pie for at least 8 hours or overnight. Let stand at room temperature about 10 minutes before serving. Serve with whipped topping and cherries. 6 to 8 servings.

NUTRITION INFORMATION PER SERVING

SERVING SIZE: 1/8 OF RECIPE		PERCENT U.S. RDA PER SERVING	
CALORIES	380	PROTEIN	6%
PROTEIN	4g	VITAMIN A	8%
CARBOHYDRATE	45g	VITAMIN C	*
FAT	21g	THIAMINE	8%
CHOLESTEROL	25mg	RIBOFLAVIN	8%
SODIUM	160 mg	NIACIN	2%
POTASSIUM	135mg	CALCIUM	6%
		IRON	4%

*Contains less than 2% of the U.S. RDA of this nutrient.

Chocolate lover's will delight in this rich cake with a creamy chocolate frosting. The frosting is easy to spread and works well when piped from a pastry tube.

French Buttercream Chocolate Cake

NUTRITION INFORMATION PER SERVING

SERVING SIZE: 1/12 OF RECIPE		PERCENT U.S. RDA PER SERVING	
CALORIES	560	PROTEIN	6%
PROTEIN	5g	VITAMIN A	8%
CARBOHYDRATE	79g	VITAMIN C	*
DIETARY FIBER	3g	THIAMINE	8%
FAT	28g	RIBOFLAVIN	10%
POLYUNSATURATED	8g	NIACIN	6%
SATURATED	11g	CALCIUM	4%
CHOLESTEROL	66mg	IRON	10%
SODIUM	460mg		
POTASSIUM	140mg		

*Contains less than 2% of the U.S. RDA of this nutrient.

CAKE

1½ cups Pillsbury's BEST® All
    Purpose or Unbleached Flour
1¼ cups sugar
½ cup unsweetened cocoa
1¼ teaspoons baking soda
1 teaspoon salt
1 cup buttermilk
⅔ cup oil
1 teaspoon vanilla
2 eggs

FROSTING

⅔ cup butter, softened
4 cups powdered sugar
2 oz. (2 squares) unsweetened
    chocolate, melted
1 teaspoon vanilla
2 to 4 tablespoons half-and-half
    or milk
    Chocolate Diamonds (see Index)
    Chocolate Shavings (see Index)

Heat oven to 350°F. Grease and flour two 8 or 9-inch round cake pans. Lightly spoon flour into measuring cup; level off. In large bowl, combine all cake ingredients at low speed until moistened; beat 3 minutes at medium speed. Pour batter into prepared pans. Bake at 350°F. for 25 to 30 minutes or until toothpick inserted in center comes out clean. Cool 5 minutes; remove from pans. Cool completely.

In large bowl, cream butter until light and fluffy. Gradually add powdered sugar, beating well after each addition. Add chocolate, beating until smooth. Add vanilla and half-and-half a tablespoon at a time; beating to desired spreading consistency. Fill and frost cake. Garnish with Chocolate Diamonds and Chocolate Shavings, or as desired. 12 servings.

HIGH ALTITUDE—Above 3500 Feet: Decrease baking soda to 1 teaspoon. Bake at 375°F. for 20 to 30 minutes.

This recipe is perfect for small families. It is made in an 8-inch square pan.

Chocolate Date Cake

CAKE

½ cup chopped dates
½ teaspoon baking soda
½ cup hot water
1 cup Pillsbury's BEST® All Purpose
    or Unbleached Flour
½ cup sugar
1 tablespoon unsweetened cocoa
¼ teaspoon salt
¼ teaspoon baking soda
½ cup margarine or butter, softened
½ teaspoon vanilla
1 egg
½ cup semi-sweet chocolate chips

TOPPING

½ cup semi-sweet chocolate chips
¼ cup chopped nuts
2 tablespoons sugar

Heat oven to 350°F. Grease and flour bottom only of 8-inch square pan. In large bowl, combine dates, ½ teaspoon baking soda and hot water; cool 5 minutes. Add remaining cake ingredients except chocolate chips to date mixture; blend at low speed until well combined. Beat 2 minutes at medium speed. Stir in ½ cup chocolate chips. Pour batter into prepared pan. Sprinkle additional ½ cup chocolate chips and nuts evenly over batter. Sprinkle with 2 tablespoons sugar. Bake at 350°F. for 25 to 35 minutes or until toothpick inserted in center comes out clean. Serve warm or cool; top with whipped cream, if desired. 6 to 8 servings.

MICROWAVE DIRECTIONS:
Lightly grease 8-inch (1½-quart) round microwave-safe dish. Prepare cake batter as directed above. Pour batter into prepared dish. Sprinkle **¼ cup** chocolate chips, ¼ cup nuts and **1 tablespoon** sugar evenly over batter. Elevate dish on inverted microwave-safe pie pan or on shelf provided. Microwave on MEDIUM for 5 to 7 minutes, rotating dish ½ turn halfway through cooking. Microwave on HIGH for 3½ to 5 minutes or until center of cake is set. Cool in dish on flat surface for 10 minutes; cool completely on wire rack.

HIGH ALTITUDE—Above 3500 Feet: Bake at 375°F. for 25 to 35 minutes.

NUTRITION INFORMATION PER SERVING

SERVING SIZE: 1/8 OF RECIPE		PERCENT U.S. RDA PER SERVING	
CALORIES	410	PROTEIN	6%
PROTEIN	4g	VITAMIN A	10%
CARBOHYDRATE	49g	VITAMIN C	*
FAT	22g	THIAMINE	8%
CHOLESTEROL	35mg	RIBOFLAVIN	6%
SODIUM	320mg	NIACIN	6%
POTASSIUM	200mg	CALCIUM	6%
		IRON	8%

*Contains less than 2% of the U.S. RDA of this nutrient.

Rich and dense, this dessert can be served with custard sauce and fresh fruit.

Chocolate Velvet Cake

3 eggs
⅔ cup sugar
¼ cup flour
4 oz. (4 squares) semi-sweet chocolate, melted
2 oz. (2 squares) unsweetened chocolate, melted
½ cup butter, melted

Heat oven to 350°F. Grease 9-inch springform pan. In large bowl, beat eggs and sugar on high speed for 2 minutes or until lemon-colored. Fold flour into egg mixture until well blended. Add chocolates and butter; stir just to combine. Pour into prepared pan. Bake at 350°F. for 25 to 35 minutes or until toothpick inserted in center comes out clean. Cool 15 minutes. Carefully remove sides of pan. Cool completely. Serve with Satin Fudge Sauce, page 84. 12 servings.

HIGH ALTITUDE—Above 3500 Feet: Decrease sugar to ½ cup.

NUTRITION INFORMATION PER SERVING

SERVING SIZE: 1/12 OF RECIPE		PERCENT U.S. RDA PER SERVING	
CALORIES	230	PROTEIN	4%
PROTEIN	3g	VITAMIN A	6%
CARBOHYDRATE	20g	VITAMIN C	*
FAT	15g	THIAMINE	*
CHOLESTEROL	90mg	RIBOFLAVIN	4%
SODIUM	95mg	NIACIN	*
POTASSIUM	90mg	CALCIUM	*
		IRON	4%

*Contains less than 2% of the U.S. RDA of this nutrient.

For those of you who love pecan pie, this is the recipe for you.

Chocolate Ribbon Pecan Pie

CRUST
- 15-oz. pkg. Pillsbury All Ready Pie Crusts
- 1 teaspoon flour

FILLING
- 8-oz. pkg. cream cheese, softened
- ⅓ cup sugar
- Dash salt
- 1 teaspoon vanilla
- 1 egg
- 1 cup chopped pecans
- ½ cup semi-sweet chocolate chips

TOPPING
- 3 eggs
- ¼ cup sugar
- 1 cup light corn syrup
- 1 teaspoon vanilla
- 1 oz. (1 square) unsweetened chocolate, melted, cooled

Heat oven to 375°F. Prepare pie crust according to package directions for **filled 1-crust pie.** (Refrigerate remaining crust for later use.) In small bowl, combine cream cheese, ⅓ cup sugar, salt, 1 teaspoon vanilla and 1 egg; mix at low speed until well blended. Spread cream cheese mixture into bottom of pie crust-lined pan. Sprinkle with pecans and chocolate chips.

In small bowl, combine all topping ingredients; mix at medium speed just until blended. Carefully pour topping over pecans and chocolate chips. Bake at 375°F. for 35 to 40 minutes or until center is set. Cool completely; store in refrigerator. Garnish as desired. 10 servings.

NUTRITION INFORMATION PER SERVING

SERVING SIZE: 1/10 OF RECIPE		PERCENT U.S. RDA PER SERVING	
CALORIES	500	PROTEIN	10%
PROTEIN	6g	VITAMIN A	8%
CARBOHYDRATE	54g	VITAMIN C	*
FAT	29g	THIAMINE	8%
CHOLESTEROL	130mg	RIBOFLAVIN	8%
SODIUM	260mg	NIACIN	*
POTASSIUM	160mg	CALCIUM	6%
		IRON	15%

*Contains less than 2% of the U.S. RDA of this nutrient.

Our taste panel was crazy about this pie! It has a tasty macaroon crust and rippled layers of chocolate and whipped cream—mmm.

Bavarian Chocolate Ripple Cream Pie

CRUST
- 1 cup finely crushed crisp coconut macaroon cookies
- ½ cup finely chopped almonds
- ⅓ cup firmly packed brown sugar
- ¼ cup flour
- ⅓ cup margarine or butter, melted

FILLING
- 1 envelope unflavored gelatin
- 1¾ cups milk
- ¾ cup sugar
- 2 oz. (2 squares) semi-sweet chocolate, chopped
- 2 tablespoons margarine or butter
- 1 teaspoon vanilla
- 1 cup whipping cream, whipped

Heat oven to 350°F. In small bowl, combine all crust ingredients. Press in bottom and up sides of 9-inch pie pan. Bake at 350°F. for 15 minutes; cool.

Soften gelatin in 1 cup of the milk for 5 minutes. In small saucepan over medium heat, combine gelatin mixture, sugar and chocolate; stir constantly just until mixture begins to boil and chocolate is melted. Remove from heat; stir in 2 tablespoons margarine until smooth. Add remaining ¾ cup milk and vanilla; mix well. Chill until almost set.

Alternately layer chocolate mixture and whipped cream in prepared crust forming 4 layers and ending with whipped cream. With spatula, gently swirl through the top 2 layers to marble. Refrigerate at least 2 hours before serving. Garnish as desired. Store any remaining pie in refrigerator. 8 servings.

NUTRITION INFORMATION PER SERVING

SERVING SIZE: 1/8 OF RECIPE		PERCENT U.S. RDA PER SERVING	
CALORIES	500	PROTEIN	10%
PROTEIN	6g	VITAMIN A	20%
CARBOHYDRATE	48g	VITAMIN C	*
FAT	32g	THIAMINE	4%
CHOLESTEROL	60mg	RIBOFLAVIN	10%
SODIUM	170mg	NIACIN	2%
POTASSIUM	290mg	CALCIUM	10%
		IRON	6%

*Contains less than 2% of the U.S. RDA of this nutrient.

Barvarian Chocolate Ripple Cream Pie

A rich, creamy filling in a delicate meringue shell.

Chocolate Mousse Angel Pie

MERINGUE SHELL
3 egg whites, room temperature
¼ teaspoon cream of tartar
Dash salt
¾ cup sugar
½ teaspoon vanilla

FILLING
6-oz. pkg. semi-sweet chocolate chips
¼ cup water
⅛ to ¼ teaspoon almond extract
1½ cups whipping cream, whipped
Toasted sliced almonds

Heat oven to 275°F. Generously butter 9-inch pie pan. In small bowl, beat egg whites, cream of tartar and salt until soft peaks form. Gradually add sugar and beat until stiff peaks form. Add vanilla; beat well. Using a metal spatula, spread meringue over the bottom and sides of prepared pan, building up the sides as high as possible. Bake at 275°F. for 1 hour. Turn oven off. Let stand in oven with door ajar for 1 hour. Remove meringue shell from oven.

In small saucepan over low heat, combine chocolate chips and water, stirring constantly until smooth. Remove from heat; stir in almond extract. Cool. Fold chocolate mixture into 2 cups of the whipped cream. Spread filling in cooled meringue shell. Store in refrigerator. Garnish with remaining whipped cream and toasted sliced almonds. 8 servings.

NUTRITION INFORMATION PER SERVING

SERVING SIZE: 1/8 OF RECIPE		PERCENT U.S. RDA PER SERVING	
CALORIES	380	PROTEIN	6%
PROTEIN	4g	VITAMIN A	10%
CARBOHYDRATE	33g	VITAMIN C	*
FAT	26g	THIAMINE	*
CHOLESTEROL	60mg	RIBOFLAVIN	6%
SODIUM	55mg	NIACIN	*
POTASSIUM	140mg	CALCIUM	4%
		IRON	4%

*Contains less than 2% of the U.S. RDA of this nutrient.

Use a wire whisk in this recipe to aid in mixing ingredients together by hand.

Sweet Chocolate Pie

CRUST
15-oz. pkg. Pillsbury All Ready Pie Crusts
1 teaspoon flour

FILLING
1 cup sugar
⅓ cup margarine or butter
4-oz. bar sweet cooking chocolate, chopped
½ cup evaporated milk or half-and-half
1 teaspoon vanilla
4 eggs
1 cup coconut
½ cup chopped pecans or walnuts
Whipped cream, if desired

Prepare pie crust according to package directions for filled one-crust pie using 9-inch pie pan. (Refrigerate remaining crust for later use.) Heat oven to 350°F.

In medium saucepan over low heat, combine sugar, margarine and chocolate, stirring constantly until smooth. Transfer chocolate mixture into medium bowl; cool 5 minutes. Add evaporated milk, vanilla and eggs; whisk until well blended. Sprinkle coconut and pecans in bottom of pie crust-lined pan; slowly pour chocolate mixture over coconut and pecans. Bake at 350°F. for 35 to 45 minutes or until center is set. Cool completely. Serve with whipped cream, if desired. 8 to 10 servings.

NUTRITION INFORMATION PER SERVING

SERVING SIZE: 1/10 OF RECIPE		PERCENT U.S. RDA PER SERVING	
CALORIES	450	PROTEIN	8%
PROTEIN	5g	VITAMIN A	10%
CARBOHYDRATE	42g	VITAMIN C	*
FAT	29g	THIAMINE	6%
CHOLESTEROL	120mg	RIBOFLAVIN	8%
SODIUM	250mg	NIACIN	*
POTASSIUM	160mg	CALCIUM	6%
		IRON	4%

*Contains less than 2% of the U.S. RDA of this nutrient.

Cranberry Chocolate Tart

PASTRY
- ⅓ cup shortening
- 1¼ cups Pillsbury's BEST® All Purpose or Unbleached Flour
- 1 teaspoon vinegar
- 2 to 4 tablespoons cold water
- ½ cup semi-sweet chocolate chips
- ¼ cup half-and-half

TOPPING*
- 2 cups fresh or frozen cranberries
- 1 cup sugar
- ½ cup water

FILLING
- 1 cup dairy sour cream
- ¾ cup milk
- 1 tablespoon grated orange peel or 2 tablespoons orange-flavored liqueur
- 3½-oz. pkg. instant vanilla pudding and pie filling mix

Heat oven to 450°F. Lightly spoon flour into measuring cup; level off. In medium bowl using pastry blender, cut shortening into flour until mixture resembles coarse crumbs. Sprinkle flour mixture with vinegar; add water, 1 tablespoon at a time, while tossing and mixing lightly with fork. Add water until dough is just moist enough to hold together.

Shape dough into ball. With floured fingers, press dough evenly over bottom and up sides of 10-inch tart pan with removable bottom or 9-inch pie pan. Flute edge, if desired. Prick bottom and sides of pastry generously with fork. Bake at 450°F. for 8 to 12 minutes or until lightly browned. In small saucepan, melt chocolate chips with half-and-half, stirring until smooth. Spread chocolate filling in bottom of baked pastry shell. Cool; refrigerate until chocolate is firm.

Meanwhile in small saucepan, combine all topping ingredients. Bring to a boil, stirring until sugar is dissolved. Boil gently 3 to 4 minutes or until most of cranberries pop. Cool at least 30 minutes.

In small bowl, combine all filling ingredients. Beat at low speed 1 minute or until blended; let stand 5 minutes. Pour over chocolate layer in baked pastry shell, spreading to cover evenly. Spoon cooled cranberries over filling, covering completely. Refrigerate at least 1 hour or until serving time. Let stand at room temperature 10 minutes before serving. 10 servings.

TIP: *One 16-oz. can whole cranberry sauce can be substituted for all topping ingredients. Place sauce in small bowl; stir gently with fork before spooning over filling.

NUTRITION INFORMATION PER SERVING

SERVING SIZE: 1/10 OF RECIPE		PERCENT U.S. RDA PER SERVING	
CALORIES	360	PROTEIN	6%
PROTEIN	4g	VITAMIN A	4%
CARBOHYDRATE	50g	VITAMIN C	4%
FAT	16g	THIAMINE	8%
CHOLESTEROL	mg	RIBOFLAVIN	8%
SODIUM	65mg	NIACIN	4%
POTASSIUM	140mg	CALCIUM	8%
		IRON	6%

COOK'S NOTE

Can different chocolate products be substituted when a recipe calls for a specific type?

On occasion, substitutes are necessary or may add a flavor variation:

- ♥ For semi-sweet chocolate chips in cookie recipes, substitute white or milk chocolate chips or chunks.

- ♥ For 1 oz. (1 square) unsweetened chocolate, use 3 tablespoons unsweetened cocoa and 1 tablespoon shortening or oil.

- ♥ For 1 oz. (1 square) semi-sweet chocolate, use 3 tablespoons semi-sweet chocolate chips or 1 oz. (1 square) unsweetened chocolate and 1 tablespoon sugar.

- ♥ For 6 oz. pkg. (1 cup) semi-sweet chocolate chips to be melted, use 6 tablespoons unsweetened cocoa, ¼ cup sugar and ¼ cup shortening.

A Pillsbury Plus Chocolate Chip Cookie Cake Mix can be substituted for the German Chocolate Cake Mix. Follow package directions to make the cake. In this recipe, the light chocolate and toffee bar flavors blend nicely.

English Toffee Crunch Cake

CAKE

1 pkg. Pillsbury Plus
    German Chocolate
    Cake Mix
1¼ cups water
⅓ cup oil
3 eggs

FROSTING

2 cups whipping cream
¼ teaspoon instant coffee
3 tablespoons firmly
    packed brown sugar
1 tablespoon chocolate-
    flavored liqueur, if
    desired
6 (1⅛ oz.) English toffee candy bars

Heat oven to 350°F. Grease and flour two 8 or 9-inch round cake pans. In large bowl, combine all cake ingredients at low speed until moistened; beat 2 minutes at **highest** speed. Pour into prepared pans. Bake at 350°F. for 25 to 35 minutes or until toothpick inserted in center comes out clean. Cool 15 minutes; remove

om pans. Cool completely.

n large bowl, beat whipping cream
nd instant coffee until slightly
nickened. Add brown sugar and
ontinue beating until stiff peaks
orm. Fold in liqueur. Split each cake
ayer in half horizontally to form
layers. Place 1 cake layer cut side up
n serving plate. Spread with ½ cup of
rosting. Crush one candy bar and
prinkle over frosting. Top with a
econd cake layer cut side down;
pread with another ½ cup of frosting.
rush one candy bar and sprinkle
ver frosting. Repeat with remaining
ayers. Frost top and sides with
emaining frosting. Coarsely chop
emaining candy bars and sprinkle on

top and sides of cake. Refrigerate until
ready to serve. Store in refrigerator.
12 servings.

HIGH ALTITUDE—Above 3500 Feet: Heat oven
to 375°F. Add 2 tablespoons flour to dry cake
mix. Bake at 375°F. for 25 to 35 minutes.

NUTRITION INFORMATION PER SERVING

SERVING SIZE: 1/12 OF RECIPE		PERCENT U.S. RDA PER SERVING	
CALORIES	520	PROTEIN	6%
PROTEIN	5g	VITAMIN A	10%
CARBOHYDRATE	43g	VITAMIN C	*
FAT	36g	THIAMINE	25%
CHOLESTEROL	120mg	RIBOFLAVIN	10%
SODIUM	390mg	NIACIN	4%
POTASSIUM	135mg	CALCIUM	8%
		IRON	8%

*Contains less than 2% of the U.S. RDA of this nutrient.

Hot fudge ice cream topping adds extra moistness to this snack cake. Serve it warm with vanilla ice cream.

Chocolate Fudge Snack Cake

CAKE
½ cup margarine or butter
1 (11.75-oz.) jar hot fudge ice cream topping
1½ cups Pillsbury's BEST® All Purpose or Unbleached Flour*
1½ cups sugar
1 cup Hungry Jack® Mashed Potato Flakes
1 teaspoon baking soda
¾ cup buttermilk**
1 teaspoon vanilla
2 eggs
1 cup finely chopped walnuts
1 (6-oz.) pkg. (1 cup) semi-sweet chocolate chips

GLAZE
½ cup sugar
¼ cup buttermilk**
¼ cup margarine or butter
1½ teaspoons light corn syrup or water
¼ teaspoon baking soda
½ teaspoon vanilla
2 tablespoons chopped walnuts

Heat oven to 350°F. Grease and flour 13x9-inch pan. In small saucepan over low heat, melt ½ cup margarine and fudge topping, stirring constantly until smooth. Lightly spoon flour into measuring cup; level off. In large bowl, combine flour and remaining cake ingredients except 1 cup walnuts and chocolate chips; beat at low speed until well blended. Add fudge mixture; beat 2 minutes at medium speed. By hand, stir in 1 cup walnuts and chocolate chips. Pour batter into greased and floured pan. Bake at 350°F. for 40 to 45 minutes or until toothpick inserted in center comes out clean.

In small saucepan, combine all glaze ingredients except vanilla and 2 table-spoons walnuts. Bring to a boil over medium heat. Reduce heat; simmer for 5 minutes or until light golden brown, stirring constantly. Remove from heat; stir in vanilla. Pour warm glaze over warm cake, spreading to cover. Sprinkle with 2 tablespoons walnuts. Serve warm or cool.
16 servings.

TIPS: *Self-rising flour is not recommended.

**To substitute for buttermilk in cake and glaze, use 1 tablespoon vinegar or lemon juice plus milk to make 1 cup. Let stand 5 minutes. Use ¾ cup for cake and ¼ cup for glaze.

HIGH ALTITUDE—Above 3500 Feet: Increase flour to 1¾ cups; decrease sugar in cake to 1 cup. Bake as directed above. Increase simmering time for glaze to 8 minutes.

NUTRITION INFORMATION PER SERVING

SERVING SIZE: 1/16 OF RECIPE		PERCENT U.S. RDA PER SERVING	
CALORIES	450	PROTEIN	8%
PROTEIN	6g	VITAMIN A	8%
CARBOHYDRATE	57g	VITAMIN C	*
FAT	22g	THIAMINE	8%
CHOLESTEROL	50mg	RIBOFLAVIN	10%
SODIUM	220mg	NIACIN	4%
POTASSIUM	210mg	CALCIUM	6%
		IRON	8%

*Contains less than 2% of the U.S. RDA of this nutrient.

Ever popular, this moist and mildly chocolate-flavored cake has a yummy broiled topping.

Cocoa Oatmeal Cake

CAKE
1¼ cups boiling water
1½ cups quick-cooking rolled oats
1½ cups Pillsbury's BEST® All Purpose or Unbleached Flour
2 tablespoons unsweetened cocoa
1 teaspoon baking soda
1 teaspoon baking powder
1 teaspoon cinnamon
Dash salt
½ cup margarine or butter, softened
1 cup firmly packed brown sugar
½ cup sugar
2 eggs
½ cup raisins

TOPPING
2 tablespoons margarine or butter, softened
¾ cup firmly packed brown sugar
2 tablespoons milk
1 cup crisp rice cereal

eat oven to 350°F. Grease and flour 3x9-inch pan. In medium bowl, combine boiling water and rolled oats; et stand 20 minutes. Lightly spoon our into measuring cup; level off. In medium bowl, combine flour, cocoa, aking soda, baking powder, innamon and salt. In large bowl, ombine margarine, brown sugar, ugar and eggs; beat until creamy. Add at mixture and flour mixture; mix vell. Stir in raisins. Spread into repared pan. Bake at 350°F. for 30 to 5 minutes or until toothpick inserted n center comes out clean.

n small bowl, combine topping ngredients; blend well. Spoon evenly ver hot cake. Broil 6 to 8 inches from eat for 1 to 2 minutes or until topping bubbly. Remove from oven. If ecessary, spread topping to cover top f cake. Cool completely. 16 servings.

IGH ALTITUDE—Above 3500 Feet: Increase our to 1½ cups plus 2 tablespoons. Bake at 75°F. for 25 to 30 minutes.

UTRITION INFORMATION PER SERVING

RVING SIZE: 16 OF RECIPE		PERCENT U.S. RDA PER SERVING	
ALORIES	290	PROTEIN	4%
ROTEIN	4g	VITAMIN A	15%
ARBOHYDRATE	49g	VITAMIN C	*
T	9g	THIAMINE	15%
HOLESTEROL	35mg	RIBOFLAVIN	10%
DIUM	300mg	NIACIN	10%
TASSIUM	180mg	CALCIUM	10%
		IRON	20%

Contains less than 2% of the U.S. RDA of this nutrient.

This recipe stores well in the refrigerator. The pudding-like frosting and tender chocolate cake have complementary flavors.

Banana Rum Fudge Cake

CAKE
1 pkg. Pillsbury Plus Dark Chocolate Cake Mix
1 cup (2 to 3 medium) mashed bananas
½ cup water
¼ cup rum*
3 eggs

FROSTING
3¾-oz. pkg. instant banana pudding and pie filling mix
1 cup cold milk
1 tablespoon rum
8-oz. container frozen whipped topping, thawed
1 oz. (1 square) semi-sweet chocolate, grated

Heat oven to 350°F. Grease and flour 13x9-inch pan. In large bowl, combine all cake ingredients; beat at medium speed for 4 minutes. Pour into prepared pan. Bake at 350°F. for 45 to 55 minutes or until toothpick inserted in center comes out clean. Cool completely.

In large bowl, combine pudding mix, milk and 1 tablespoon rum; beat at medium speed until thick. Fold in whipped topping. Spread evenly over cooled cake; sprinkle with grated chocolate. Cover; store in refrigerator. 12 servings.

TIP: *If desired, 1 teaspoon rum extract can be substituted for the rum in the cake. Increase water to ¾ cup. One-fourth teaspoon rum extract can be substituted for the rum in the frosting.

HIGH ALTITUDE—Above 3500 Feet: Add 3 tablespoons flour to dry cake mix. Bake as directed above.

NUTRITION INFORMATION PER SERVING

SERVING SIZE: 1/12 OF RECIPE		PERCENT U.S. RDA PER SERVING	
CALORIES	350	PROTEIN	6%
PROTEIN	5g	VITAMIN A	2%
CARBOHYDRATE	52g	VITAMIN C	2%
FAT	12g	THIAMINE	8%
CHOLESTEPOL	70mg	RIBOFLAVIN	10%
SODIUM	430mg	NIACIN	4%
POTASSIUM	200mg	CALCIUM	15%
		IRON	10%

Boston Creme Cake

CAKE

1 pkg. Pillsbury Yellow
   Cake Mix
1 cup water
⅓ cup oil
3 eggs

FILLING

3 oz. pkg. vanilla or French vanilla
   pudding and pie filling
1¾ cups milk

TOPPING

1 cup fudge topping

Heat oven to 350°F. Grease and flour
two 8 or 9-inch round cake pans. In
large bowl, combine all cake
ingredients at low speed until
moistened; beat 2 minutes at **highest**
speed. Pour into prepared pans. Bake
at 350°F. for 25 to 35 minutes or until
toothpick inserted in center comes
out clean. Cool 15 minutes; remove
from pans. Cool completely.

In medium saucepan, combine all
filling ingredients. Cook over medium
heat until mixture comes to a full boil,
stirring constantly. Remove from heat.
Cover surface with plastic wrap;
refrigerate until thickened.

Split one cake layer in half
horizontally, forming 2 layers. Spread
half of the filling over bottom layer.
Place top layer over filling. Repeat
with remaining cake layer and filling.
Heat fudge topping in small saucepan
over low heat until softened. Pour and
spread over top of filled cakes,
allowing topping to drizzle down
sides. Garnish as desired. Store any
remaining cake in refrigerator.
16 servings.

🖾 **MICROWAVE DIRECTIONS:**
Prepare cake as directed. In small
microwave-safe bowl, combine all
filling ingredients. Microwave on
HIGH for 4 to 5 minutes, stirring once
halfway through cooking. Cover
surface with plastic wrap; refrigerate
until thickened.

In small microwave-safe bowl,
microwave topping on HIGH for 15 to
30 seconds to soften. Fill and top cakes
as directed.

HIGH ALTITUDE—Above 3500 Feet: Add ⅓ cup
flour to dry cake mix and increase water by
2 tablespoons. Bake as directed above.

NUTRITION INFORMATION PER SERVING

SERVING SIZE: 1/16 OF RECIPE		PERCENT U.S. RDA PER SERVING	
CALORIES	280	PROTEIN	6%
PROTEIN	4g	VITAMIN A	2%
CARBOHYDRATE	42g	VITAMIN C	*
DIETARY FIBER	2g	THIAMINE	6%
FAT	12g	RIBOFLAVIN	10%
POLYUNSATURATED	3g	NIACIN	4%
SATURATED	4g	CALCIUM	10%
CHOLESTEROL	42mg	IRON	4%
SODIUM	260mg		
POTASSIUM	130mg		
*Contains less than 2% of the U.S. RDA of this nutrient.			

German Apple Cake

CAKE

4 cups (4 to 5 medium) thinly
   sliced, peeled apples
1 pkg. Pillsbury Plus German
   Chocolate Cake Mix
2 teaspoons cinnamon
1¼ cups water
¼ cup margarine or butter,
   softened
3 eggs
½ cup chopped nuts

FROSTING

3-oz. pkg. cream cheese, softened
2 tablespoons margarine or
   butter, softened
1½ cups powdered sugar
½ teaspoon cinnamon
½ teaspoon vanilla
1 to 2 tablespoons milk

Heat oven to 350°F. Spread apples
evenly in ungreased 13x9-inch pan. In
large bowl, blend cake mix, cinnamon,
water, margarine and eggs at low
speed until moistened; beat 2 minutes
at **highest** speed. Stir in nuts. Pour
batter evenly over apples. Bake at
350°F. for 40 to 50 minutes or until
toothpick inserted in center comes
out clean. Cool completely. In small
bowl, blend frosting ingredients until
smooth. Frost cooled cake. Store in
refrigerator. 12 servings.

HIGH ALTITUDE—Above 3500 Feet: Add
2 tablespoons flour to dry cake mix. Bake at
375°F. for 40 to 45 minutes.

NUTRITION INFORMATION PER SERVING

SERVING SIZE: 1/12 OF RECIPE		PERCENT U.S. RDA PER SERVING	
CALORIES	400	PROTEIN	8%
PROTEIN	5g	VITAMIN A	8%
CARBOHYDRATE	56g	VITAMIN C	2%
FAT	17g	THIAMINE	10%
CHOLESTEROL	80mg	RIBOFLAVIN	8%
SODIUM	420mg	NIACIN	4%
POTASSIUM	160mg	CALCIUM	6%
		IRON	8%

Pictured top to bottom: Spiral Chocolate Jam Tart p. 73, White Chocolate Cherry Tart

A dazzling dessert made with trendy white chocolate.

White Chocolate Cherry Tart

CRUST

15 oz. pkg. Pillsbury All Ready Pie Crusts
1 teaspoon flour
2 teaspoons sugar

FILLING

½ cup powdered sugar
½ cup butter or margarine, softened
5 oz. bar Alpine White candy bar with chopped almonds, melted, cooled
⅓ cup whipping cream
21 oz. can cherry fruit pie filling
White Chocolate Curls (see Index)

Heat oven to 450°F. Prepare pie crust according to package directions for **unfilled one-crust pie** using 10-inch tart pan with removable bottom. (Refrigerate remaining crust for later use.) Place prepared crust in pan; press in bottom and up sides of pan. Trim edges if necessary. Sprinkle with sugar. Generously prick crust with fork. Bake at 450°F. for 9 to 11 minutes or until lightly browned. Cool.

In small bowl, beat powdered sugar and butter until light and fluffy. Blend in melted white chocolate; mix well. Add whipping cream; beat well. Spread filling over prepared crust. Refrigerate about 1 hour before serving. To serve, spoon cherry filling over each wedge; garnish with White Chocolate Curls. Store in refrigerator. 10 servings.

NUTRITION INFORMATION PER SERVING

SERVING SIZE: 1/10 OF RECIPE		PERCENT U.S. RDA PER SERVING	
CALORIES	430	PROTEIN	4%
PROTEIN	3g	VITAMIN A	10%
CARBOHYDRATE	53g	VITAMIN C	4%
DIETARY FIBER	0g	THIAMINE	*
FAT	24g	RIBOFLAVIN	6%
POLYUNSATURATED	2g	NIACIN	*
SATURATED	13g	CALCIUM	4%
CHOLESTEROL	44mg	IRON	2%
SODIUM	220mg		
POTASSIUM	135mg		

*Contains less than 2% of the U.S. RDA of this nutrient.

A ganache is basically a mixture of whipping cream, chocolate and margarine that is melted, cooled and whipped. It's so simple, yet a new, trendy technique to a luscious, light filling.

Ganache Layered Cream Torte

CAKE

1 pkg. Pillsbury Plus Devil's Food Cake Mix
1 cup dairy sour cream
¾ cup water
⅓ cup oil
3 eggs
1 cup miniature semi-sweet chocolate chips

FILLING

1½ cups whipping cream
8 oz. (8 squares) semi-sweet chocolate, chopped
¼ cup margarine or butter
Chocolate Curls (see Index)
Powdered sugar

Heat oven to 350°F. Grease and flour two 9-inch round cake pans. In large bowl, combine cake mix, sour cream, water, oil and eggs at low speed until moistened. Beat 2 minutes at **highest** speed. Stir in chocolate chips. Pour batter into prepared pans. Bake at 350°F. for 35 to 45 minutes or until toothpick inserted in center comes out clean. Cool 15 minutes; remove from pans. Cool completely.

In medium saucepan over medium heat, combine whipping cream, chocolate and margarine, stirring constantly until mixture is smooth and begins to boil. Remove from heat. Refrigerate for at least 1 hour or until well chilled. With hand mixer, beat chocolate mixture until light and fluffy.

Split each cake layer in half horizontally to form 4 layers. Place 1 cake layer cut side up on serving plate. Spread with ¼ of filling mixture. Top with a second cake layer cut side down; spread with another ¼ of filling. Repeat with remaining layers. Spread remaining filling over top of torte.

Garnish with Large Chocolate Curls and powdered sugar. Refrigerate; let stand at room temperature about 10 minutes before serving. 16 servings

HIGH ALTITUDE—Above 3500 Feet: Add 3 tablespoons flour to dry cake mix. Bake at 375° for 40 to 45 minutes.

NUTRITION INFORMATION PER SERVING

SERVING SIZE: 1/16 OF RECIPE		PERCENT U.S. RDA PER SERVING	
CALORIES	510	PROTEIN	8%
PROTEIN	5g	VITAMIN A	10%
CARBOHYDRATE	44g	VITAMIN C	*
FAT	35g	THIAMINE	6%
CHOLESTEROL	90mg	RIBOFLAVIN	8%
SODIUM	330mg	NIACIN	4%
POTASSIUM	210mg	CALCIUM	10%
		IRON	8%

*Contains less than 2% of the U.S. RDA of this nutrient.

COOK'S NOTE

What is white chocolate?

White chocolate, according to the Food and Drug Administration, is really not chocolate at all because it does not contain "chocolate liquor" from the cocoa bean. It is a blend of cocoa butter, sugar, milk and flavorings.

White chocolate is also available in different forms:

♥ *Imported varieties in bar form*
♥ *Vanilla-flavored candy coating or compound chocolate*
♥ *Vanilla-milk flavored chips*

The imported European varieties are made with cocoa butter. Candy coating, compound chocolate and chips are made with coconut, soybean or palm kernel oils.

White chocolate has a mild flavor similar to milk chocolate. It can be found in specialty food shops and the baking section of some supermarkets.

This dessert is a showstopper! It can be made with any flavor of jam you may have on hand.

Spiral Chocolate Jam Tart

CRUST
15-oz. pkg. Pillsbury All Ready Pie
      Crusts
1 teaspoon flour

FILLING
¼ cup sugar
¾ cup whipping cream
4 egg yolks
6 oz. (6 squares) semi-sweet
      chocolate, chopped
2 tablespoons butter or
      margarine, softened
1 tablespoon vanilla
½ cup apricot, strawberry or
      raspberry jam
2 oz. white chocolate or vanilla-
      flavored candy coating

Heat oven to 450°F. Prepare pie crust according to package directions for **unfilled one-crust pie** using 10-inch tart pan with removable bottom. Refrigerate remaining crust for later use.) Place prepared crust in pan; press in bottom and up sides of pan. Trim edges if necessary. Generously prick crust with fork. Bake at 450°F. for 9 to 11 minutes or until lightly browned. Cool.

In small saucepan over low heat, combine sugar, whipping cream and egg yolks, stirring constantly until mixture begins to thicken, about 5 to 10 minutes. Remove from heat; stir in chocolate, butter and vanilla until mixture is smooth. Cool slightly. Spread jam over prepared crust. Spread chocolate mixture over jam layer.

In small saucepan over low heat, melt white chocolate, stirring constantly until smooth. Cool slightly. Spoon white chocolate into pastry bag with writing tip. Starting from the center of tart working outward, pipe a spiral circle of white chocolate on top of tart. Working from the center of the spiral to the outer edges, draw the blade of a small knife lightly through the chocolate spiral to create a feathering effect. Wipe knife clean after each line to ensure a clean design. Garnish as desired. Store in refrigerator.
16 servings.

NUTRITION INFORMATION PER SERVING

SERVING SIZE: 1/16 OF RECIPE		PERCENT U.S. RDA PER SERVING	
CALORIES	250	PROTEIN	2%
PROTEIN	2g	VITAMIN A	6%
CARBOHYDRATE	24g	VITAMIN C	*
FAT	16g	THIAMINE	*
CHOLESTEROL	90mg	RIBOFLAVIN	2%
SODIUM	105mg	NIACIN	*
POTASSIUM	75mg	CALCIUM	2%
		IRON	4%

*Contains less than 2% of the U.S. RDA of this nutrient.

Chocolate Potpourri

*Clockwise from left: Cherry-Chocolate Drink p. 77, Hot Chocolate Malt p. 78,
Marshmallowy Chocolate Milk p. 77*

Chocolate Potpourri

A *sweet sampler to savor and sip.*

Melt-in-your-mouth morsels, satiny sauces and some very satisfying sipping — all star royally rich chocolate. If your holidays were too hectic for candy making, this month's slower pace may inspire you to try some of these spectacular sweets.

To remove any guesswork, some of our recipes suggest using a candy thermometer. A few require a pastry bag — great fun to use and inexpensive to purchase. Other confections, like Microwave Nut Goodie Bars and Milk Chocolate Peanut Butter Bark, are as foolproof as recipes can be. Our Valentine's Day gift ideas are sure to capture the hearts of family and friends. Elegant white chocolate makes fanciful and distinctive White Chocolate-Covered Cherries, White and Dark Chocolate Cut Outs and a unique White Chocolate Lace Basket. Microwave instructions are included wherever practical, and because proper storage of candies is so important, we have added tips to keep these treats at their peak of freshness and flavor to the last bite.

Two scrumptious sauce selections will become year-round favorites for you to serve over ice cream, pound cake, plain puddings, fresh fruits or combined with other ingredients for party-perfect parfaits. They are, of course, make-ahead so you can have them on hand in the refrigerator for impromptu snacks and desserts.

Microwavable Single-Serving Hot Beverages

Enjoy piping hot pleasures to warm hands and hearts from sunup to sundown. They are ready in minutes with microwave heating for speedy serving at breakfast, break-time, after dinner and at bedtime.

Some tips for trouble-free preparation? **Use only microwave-safe cups and mugs.** Avoid fine china, questionable plastics and containers with metal trim or with paints and glazes containing metallic substances. If you are uncertain about a serving container's microwavability, use a glass measure for heating the drink and then pour it into the serving cup.

Remember you are heating, not cooking, ingredients. Therefore, it is important to **watch timing carefully.** Begin with the least amount of time in the suggested range and add seconds in intervals if necessary.

Avoid boilovers by using a cup, mug or other container **large enough** to allow for some bubbling, should that occur. Our recipes were tested in mugs with a capacity of 10 ounces and in 650-watt ovens. When increasing amounts for several servings, you may want to heat mixtures in a microwave-safe glass measure, snifter, jar, bowl, pitcher or casserole dish.

Cherry-Chocolate Drink

MICROWAVE DIRECTIONS: In microwave-safe mug, combine ¾ cup milk, 2 tablespoons chocolate syrup and 1 tablespoon maraschino cherry juice. Microwave on HIGH for 2 to 2½ minutes or until hot. Serve with 2 tablespoons whipped cream and long-stemmed maraschino cherry. 1 serving.

NUTRITION INFORMATION PER SERVING

SERVING SIZE: 1 SERVING		PERCENT U.S. RDA PER SERVING	
CALORIES	270	PROTEIN	10%
PROTEIN	7g	VITAMIN A	10%
CARBOHYDRATE	38g	VITAMIN C	2%
FAT	10g	THIAMINE	4%
CHOLESTEROL	35mg	RIBOFLAVIN	20%
SODIUM	115mg	NIACIN	*
POTASSIUM	420mg	CALCIUM	25%
		IRON	4%

*Contains less than 2% of the U.S. RDA of this nutrient.

Café au Lait

MICROWAVE DIRECTIONS: In microwave-safe mug, combine ½ cup strong coffee, ½ cup milk and 2 tablespoons chocolate syrup. Microwave on HIGH for 2 to 2½ minutes or until hot. Serve with 2 tablespoons whipped cream and sprinkle with cinnamon. 1 serving.

NUTRITION INFORMATION PER SERVING

SERVING SIZE: 1 SERVING		PERCENT U.S. RDA PER SERVING	
CALORIES	220	PROTEIN	8%
PROTEIN	5g	VITAMIN A	8%
CARBOHYDRATE	30g	VITAMIN C	*
FAT	9g	THIAMINE	2%
CHOLESTEROL	30mg	RIBOFLAVIN	15%
SODIUM	85mg	NIACIN	2%
POTASSIUM	340mg	CALCIUM	15%
		IRON	4%

*Contains less than 2% of the U.S. RDA of this nutrient.

Marshmallowy Chocolate Milk

MICROWAVE DIRECTIONS: In large microwave-safe mug, combine 1 cup chocolate milk and 2 tablespoons marshmallow creme. Microwave on HIGH for 2 to 2½ minutes or until hot. Stir to dissolve marshmallow creme. Serve with 2 tablespoons of marshmallow creme and sprinkle with miniature chocolate chips. 1 serving.

NUTRITION INFORMATION PER SERVING

SERVING SIZE: 1 SERVING		PERCENT U.S. RDA PER SERVING	
CALORIES	300	PROTEIN	10%
PROTEIN	8g	VITAMIN A	10%
CARBOHYDRATE	51g	VITAMIN C	4%
FAT	7g	THIAMINE	6%
CHOLESTEROL	15mg	RIBOFLAVIN	25%
SODIUM	160mg	NIACIN	*
POTASSIUM	440mg	CALCIUM	30%
		IRON	4%

*Contains less than 2% of the U.S. RDA of this nutrient.

Hot Chocolate Malt

~⨯~

■ **MICROWAVE DIRECTIONS:** In microwave-safe mug, combine 1 cup chocolate milk and 2 teaspoons chocolate malted milk powder. Microwave on HIGH for 2 to 2½ minutes or until hot. Stir until smooth. Serve with a scoop of vanilla ice cream. 1 serving.

NUTRITION INFORMATION PER SERVING

SERVING SIZE: 1 SERVING		PERCENT U.S. RDA PER SERVING	
CALORIES	330	PROTEIN	15%
PROTEIN	11g	VITAMIN A	15%
CARBOHYDRATE	45g	VITAMIN C	2%
FAT	12g	THIAMINE	8%
CHOLESTEROL	45mg	RIBOFLAVIN	35%
SODIUM	220mg	NIACIN	2%
POTASSIUM	570mg	CALCIUM	35%
		IRON	4%

Café Amaretto

~⨯~

■ **MICROWAVE DIRECTIONS:** In microwave-safe mug, combine ¾ cup strong coffee and 2 tablespoons chocolate syrup. Microwave on HIGH for 2 to 2½ minutes or until hot. Stir in 1 tablespoon almond-flavored liqueur. Serve with 2 tablespoons whipped cream and sprinkle with Grated Chocolate (see Index). 1 serving.

NUTRITION INFORMATION PER SERVING

SERVING SIZE: 1 SERVING		PERCENT U.S. RDA PER SERVING	
CALORIES	210	PROTEIN	*
PROTEIN	1g	VITAMIN A	4%
CARBOHYDRATE	37g	VITAMIN C	*
FAT	7g	THIAMINE	*
CHOLESTEROL	20mg	RIBOFLAVIN	*
SODIUM	25mg	NIACIN	2%
POTASSIUM	180mg	CALCIUM	*
		IRON	4%

*Contains less than 2% of the U.S. RDA of this nutrient.

Mocha Frosted Coffee

~⨯~

■ **MICROWAVE DIRECTIONS:** In microwave-safe mug, combine ¾ cup strong coffee and 2 tablespoons half-and-half. Microwave on HIGH for 2 to 2½ minutes or until hot. Stir in 1 tablespoon Irish creme liqueur. Serve with 2 tablespoons whipped cream and sprinkle with Chocolate Shavings (see Index). 1 serving.

NUTRITION INFORMATION PER SERVING

SERVING SIZE: 1 SERVING		PERCENT U.S. RDA PER SERVING	
CALORIES	160	PROTEIN	2%
PROTEIN	1g	VITAMIN A	6%
CARBOHYDRATE	15g	VITAMIN C	*
FAT	10g	THIAMINE	*
CHOLESTEROL	30mg	RIBOFLAVIN	2%
SODIUM	20mg	NIACIN	2%
POTASSIUM	110mg	CALCIUM	4%
		IRON	

*Contains less than 2% of the U.S. RDA of this nutrient.

Café Israel

~⨯~

■ **MICROWAVE DIRECTIONS:** In microwave-safe mug, combine 2 squares (⅛ bar) chopped sweet cooking chocolate, 1 cup water, 1 teaspoon instant coffee and 2 strips orange peel. Microwave on HIGH for 2 to 3 minutes or until boiling. Let steep 1 minute; stir. Strain through fine sieve to remove orange peel and undissolved chocolate. Serve with 2 tablespoons whipped cream. 1 servings.

NUTRITION INFORMATION PER SERVING

SERVING SIZE: 1 SERVING		PERCENT U.S. RDA PER SERVING	
CALORIES	90	PROTEIN	*
PROTEIN	1g	VITAMIN A	4%
CARBOHYDRATE	4g	VITAMIN C	*
FAT	8g	THIAMINE	*
CHOLESTEROL	20mg	RIBOFLAVIN	*
SODIUM	10mg	NIACIN	*
POTASSIUM	55mg	CALCIUM	*
		IRON	*

*Contains less than 2% of the U.S. RDA of this nutrient.

Frosty Chocolate Nog

~⨯~

■ **MICROWAVE DIRECTIONS:** In microwave-safe mug, combine ¾ cup milk and 1 tablespoon sweetened cocoa drink mix. Microwave on HIGH for 2 to 2½ minutes or until hot. Stir in 1 scoop of chocolate ice cream until frothy. 1 serving.

NUTRITION INFORMATION PER SERVING

SERVING SIZE: 1 SERVING		PERCENT U.S. RDA PER SERVING	
CALORIES	250	PROTEIN	10%
PROTEIN	9g	VITAMIN A	10%
CARBOHYDRATE	29g	VITAMIN C	2%
FAT	11g	THIAMINE	6%
CHOLESTEROL	45mg	RIBOFLAVIN	25%
SODIUM	160mg	NIACIN	*
POTASSIUM	440mg	CALCIUM	30%
		IRON	*

*Contains less than 2% of the U.S. RDA of this nutrient.

Who can resist a flavorful, chewy, melt-in-your-mouth caramel?

Chocolate Caramel Diamonds

1 cup butter
1¼ cups sugar
1 cup firmly packed brown sugar
1 cup light corn syrup
14-oz. can sweetened condensed milk
2 oz. (2 squares) semi-sweet chocolate, chopped
2 teaspoons vanilla

Line 9-inch square pan with foil; butter foil. In medium heavy saucepan over low heat, melt butter. Add sugar, brown sugar and corn syrup. Cook over medium low heat until sugar dissolves and mixture is well blended, stirring constantly. Stir in sweetened condensed milk. Cook over medium heat, stirring constantly until mixture reaches 230°F. on candy thermometer, about 30 minutes. Stir in chocolate; cook until mixture reaches soft-ball stage (240°F.), about 15 minutes. Remove from heat; stir in vanilla. Pour into prepared pan; cool. Refrigerate several hours or until candy is set. Remove from pan; peel away foil. Cut into diamond shapes or squares. Store in covered container.
2 lb. 12 oz. candy.

NUTRITION INFORMATION PER SERVING

SERVING SIZE: 1 OUNCE		PERCENT U.S. RDA PER SERVING	
CALORIES	140	PROTEIN	*
PROTEIN	1g	VITAMIN A	4%
CARBOHYDRATE	22g	VITAMIN C	*
FAT	5g	THIAMINE	*
CHOLESTEROL	15mg	RIBOFLAVIN	2%
SODIUM	60mg	NIACIN	*
POTASSIUM	60mg	CALCIUM	2%
		IRON	2%

*Contains less than 2% of the U.S. RDA of this nutrient.

One of our taste panel's favorite candies. A buttery, crunchy, flavorful candy made to perfection with a candy thermometer.

Chocolate Cashew Buttercrunch

BUTTERCRUNCH
1 cup butter
2 tablespoons light corn syrup
2 tablespoons water
1 cup sugar
1 cup finely chopped cashews

TOPPING
6-oz. pkg. (1 cup) semi-sweet chocolate chips
½ cup coarsely chopped cashews

Line jelly roll pan with foil; butter foil. In heavy 2-quart saucepan over medium heat, combine butter, corn syrup, water and sugar, stirring constantly until sugar dissolves and mixture boils. Using candy thermometer, continue cooking to soft-crack stage (290°F.), stirring only as needed to prevent sticking. Remove from heat. Quickly stir in 1 cup cashews. Pour mixture into prepared pan. Let stand 2 to 3 minutes to harden.

Sprinkle with chocolate chips; let stand 2 minutes to soften. Spread evenly over buttercrunch. Sprinkle ½ cup cashews over chocolate. Refrigerate until chocolate is firm; break into pieces. Store in covered container. 1 lb. 12 oz. candy.

NUTRITION INFORMATION PER SERVING

SERVING SIZE: 1 OUNCE		PERCENT U.S. RDA PER SERVING	
CALORIES	170	PROTEIN	2%
PROTEIN	2g	VITAMIN A	4%
CARBOHYDRATE	14g	VITAMIN C	*
FAT	12g	THIAMINE	*
CHOLESTEROL	20mg	RIBOFLAVIN	*
SODIUM	120mg	NIACIN	*
POTASSIUM	65mg	CALCIUM	*
		IRON	4%

*Contains less than 2% of the U.S. RDA of this nutrient.

Microwave Nut Goodie Bars

For an extra chocolaty bar, use milk chocolate pudding instead of vanilla.

Microwave Nut Goodie Bars

12-oz. pkg. (2 cups) semi-sweet chocolate chips
12-oz. pkg. (2 cups) butterscotch chips
2 cups peanut butter
2 cups salted peanuts
1 cup margarine or butter
3⅛-oz. pkg. vanilla or milk chocolate pudding and pie filling mix (not instant)
½ cup evaporated milk
2-lb. bag (7½ cups) **sifted** powdered sugar*
1 teaspoon vanilla

▪ MICROWAVE DIRECTIONS:
Butter 15x10-inch jelly roll pan. In medium microwave-safe bowl, combine chocolate chips and butterscotch chips. Microwave on MEDIUM for 6 to 7 minutes, stirring every 2 minutes. Stir until smooth. Stir in peanut butter; mix well. Spread half of mixture into prepared pan; refrigerate. Stir peanuts into remaining chocolate mixture; set aside.

In large microwave-safe bowl, place margarine. Microwave on HIGH 15 to 60 seconds or until melted. Stir in pudding mix and evaporated milk; blend well. Microwave on HIGH for 45 to 60 seconds or until hot. DO NOT BOIL. Stir in powdered sugar and vanilla. Carefully spread over chocolate layer. Refrigerate 30 minutes to set. Drop remaining chocolate-peanut mixture by tablespoonful over chilled pudding layer. Carefully spread to cover. Refrigerate until firm; cut into bars. Store in covered container in refrigerator. 60 bars.

TIP: *For the success of this recipe, sift powdered sugar.

Use any shape pan, mold or cookie cutters to create a pretty lace basket container. Melt candy coating proportionally to pan size. In this recipe, 6 oz. candy coating is used for an 8-inch pan.

White Chocolate Lace Basket

6 oz. vanilla-flavored candy coating or almond bark, melted

Press a piece of foil firmly over outside of heart-shaped, 8-inch cake pan. Place pan in freezer.

In small saucepan over low heat, melt candy coating, stirring constantly until smooth. Cool slightly. Pour melted coating into small squeeze bottle or pastry bag fitted with small writing tip. Drizzle coating randomly over bottom and sides of foil-covered pan; apply heavier coating on edges and corners. Freeze pan for 30 minutes.

Unmold by **carefully** lifting foil from pan. **Carefully** peel foil away from chocolate. Place on tray. Refrigerate until ready to use. Fill with candy or cookies. 1 basket.

TIP: If basket breaks, mend with melted candy coating.

Pictured top to bottom: Milk Chocolate Peanut Butter Bark p. 85,
White Chocolate-Covered Cherries p. 84, White Chocolate Lace Basket p. 81

Pictured top to bottom: Chocolate Caramel Diamonds p. 79,
White and Dark Chocolate Cutouts p. 84, White Chocolate Lace Basket p. 81.

The fondant in this recipe ripens or liquifies in about 2 weeks, so you will need to make this recipe in advance. For an extra special gift, make a small White Chocolate Lace Basket (see Index) and fill it with these tempting confections.

White Chocolate-Covered Cherries

2 (10-oz.) jars maraschino cherries
    with stems
¼ cup butter, softened
1 tablespoon cherry-
    flavored liqueur
1 tablespoon light corn
    syrup
2 cups powdered sugar
1½ lb. vanilla-flavored candy
    coating, chopped

Drain cherries; let dry on paper towel overnight. In small bowl, combine butter, liqueur and corn syrup. Stir in powdered sugar; knead until smooth. Form a heaping ½ teaspoonful fondant around each cherry. Place on waxed paper-covered cookie sheet; refrigerate.

In small saucepan over low heat, melt candy coating, stirring constantly until smooth. Remove from heat; set over pan of hot water. Holding cherries by the stems, dip quickly into the melted coating. Be sure to completely cover; set on waxed paper-covered cookie sheet. Refrigerate for 30 minutes to set coating. Dip each coated cherry a second time in coating. It may be necessary to reheat coating over low heat. Refrigerate double dipped cherries to set coating. Store in covered container at room temperature for 2 weeks to allow cherries to ripen. 40 cherries.

NUTRITION INFORMATION PER SERVING

SERVING SIZE: 1 CHERRY		PERCENT U.S. RDA PER SERVING	
CALORIES	130	PROTEIN	*
PROTEIN	1g	VITAMIN A	*
CARBOHYDRATE	17g	VITAMIN C	*
FAT	7g	THIAMINE	*
CHOLESTEROL	2mg	RIBOFLAVIN	*
SODIUM	15mg	NIACIN	*
POTASSIUM	55mg	CALCIUM	*
		IRON	2%

*Contains less than 2% of the U.S. RDA of this nutrient.

Follow recipe directions for "tempering" chocolate. This simple technique will prevent "bloom" or discoloration of the chocolate.

White and Dark Chocolate Cutouts

3 oz. white chocolate, chopped
6 oz. (6 squares) semi-sweet
    chocolate, chopped

Temper white chocolate by melting 2 oz. in a double boiler. Melt just until the white chocolate is smooth (110 to 120°F.) Remove from heat; stir in remaining 1 oz. white chocolate until it becomes smooth. Set aside.

Temper semi-sweet chocolate by melting 4 oz. in a double boiler. Melt just until the chocolate is smooth (110 to 120°F.) Remove from heat; stir in remaining 2 oz. chocolate until it becomes smooth.

Pour melted semi-sweet chocolate onto waxed paper-covered cookie sheet, spreading to ⅛-inch thickness. Reserve about 2 tablespoons for garnish design. Refrigerate until slightly hardened, about 10 minutes. Press hors d'oeuvre or small cookie cutters firmly into chocolate. Spoon a small amount of white chocolate in center of each cutout; spread almost to edge.

Drizzle with remaining semi-sweet chocolate. Refrigerate until slightly hardened. Lift gently from waxed paper with spatula. Store candy between layers of waxed paper in covered container in refrigerator. 8 oz. candy (about 5 dozen pieces).

NUTRITION INFORMATION PER SERVING

SERVING SIZE: 1/2 OUNCE		PERCENT U.S. RDA PER SERVING	
CALORIES	90	PROTEIN	*
PROTEIN	1g	VITAMIN A	*
CARBOHYDRATE	9g	VITAMIN C	*
FAT	6g	THIAMINE	*
CHOLESTEROL	2mg	RIBOFLAVIN	*
SODIUM	0mg	NIACIN	*
POTASSIUM	50mg	CALCIUM	*
		IRON	2%

*Contains less than 2% of the U.S. RDA of this nutrient.

COOK'S NOTE

How and why do you temper chocolate?

Why is it necessary to temper chocolate?

Chocolate contains cocoa butter which is made up of fat crystals. Some of the fat crystals may recrystalize if you melt and cool chocolate without tempering it, forming dull gray streaks called bloom. Tempering chocolate prevents bloom.

How is chocolate tempered?
Tempering is basically a method of melting and cooling chocolate to eliminate gray streaks from forming. It also keeps chocolate firm and glossy at room temperature. To temper, chop chocolate into small pieces. Place 2/3 of the chopped chocolate in the top of a double boiler over hot water. Over medium heat, melt chocolate stirring constantly until mixture reaches 110 to 120°F. Be careful that no moisture gets into the chocolate. Add remaining 1/3 chopped chocolate. Remove from heat and stir until smooth.

The creamiest, thickest, richest and nuttiest fudge imaginable.

Macadamia Fudge

2 cups sugar
¼ teaspoon salt
⅔ cup evaporated milk
¼ cup butter
11.5-oz. pkg. milk chocolate chips
2 oz. (2 squares) unsweetened chocolate, chopped
4 cups miniature marshmallows
2 teaspoons vanilla
1 cup chopped macadamia nuts

Line 8-inch square pan with foil. In large heavy saucepan over medium heat, combine sugar, salt, evaporated milk and butter, stirring constantly until mixture comes to a full rolling boil. Boil 6 minutes, stirring frequently. Remove from heat; stir in milk chocolate chips, chocolate, marshmallows and vanilla; blend until smooth. Stir in macadamia nuts. Pour into prepared pan. Refrigerate about 2 hours. Remove from pan; peel away foil. Cut into squares.
2 lb. 10½ oz. candy.

NUTRITION INFORMATION PER SERVING

SERVING SIZE: 1 OUNCE		PERCENT U.S. RDA PER SERVING	
CALORIES	140	PROTEIN	*
PROTEIN	1g	VITAMIN A	*
CARBOHYDRATE	19g	VITAMIN C	*
FAT	7g	THIAMINE	*
CHOLESTEROL	2mg	RIBOFLAVIN	*
SODIUM	30mg	NIACIN	*
POTASSIUM	55mg	CALCIUM	2%
		IRON	*

*Contains less than 2% of the U.S. RDA of this nutrient.

Milk Chocolate Peanut Butter Bark

6 oz. (1 cup) milk chocolate chips
6 oz. (1 cup) peanut butter chips
½ cup chopped salted peanuts

Line 13x9-inch pan with foil. In medium saucepan over low heat, melt milk chocolate chips and peanut butter chips, stirring constantly until smooth. Stir in peanuts. Pour into prepared pan; spread. Refrigerate for about 1 hour. Before serving, break into pieces. Store in covered container in refrigerator. About 1 lb. candy.

MICROWAVE DIRECTIONS: In medium microwave-safe bowl, combine milk chocolate chips and peanut butter chips. Microwave on MEDIUM for 2 minutes; stir. Microwave on MEDIUM an additional 2 minutes; stir until melted. Stir in peanuts. Follow as directed above.

NUTRITION INFORMATION PER SERVING

SERVING SIZE: 1 OUNCE		PERCENT U.S. RDA PER SERVING	
CALORIES	150	PROTEIN	6%
PROTEIN	4g	VITAMIN A	*
CARBOHYDRATE	12g	VITAMIN C	*
FAT	9g	THIAMINE	*
CHOLESTEROL	0mg	RIBOFLAVIN	*
SODIUM	45mg	NIACIN	8%
POTASSIUM	115mg	CALCIUM	2%
		IRON	2%

*Contains less than 2% of the U.S. RDA of this nutrient.

This recipe makes almost 2 cups of sauce and stores well refrigerated in a covered container.

Satin Fudge Sauce

4 oz. (4 squares) semi-sweet
  chocolate, chopped
⅓ cup butter or margarine
1½ cups powdered sugar
5⅓-oz. can evaporated milk
1 teaspoon vanilla

In medium heavy saucepan over medium heat, combine all ingredients except vanilla, stirring constantly until mixture boils. Reduce heat to low; cook 5 minutes, stirring constantly. Remove from heat; stir in vanilla. Serve warm over ice cream or desserts. Cover; store in refrigerator. 1⅔ cups.

▆ MICROWAVE DIRECTIONS: In medium microwave-safe bowl, combine all ingredients except vanilla. Microwave on HIGH for 4 to 5 minutes or until mixture begins to boil, stirring every 2 minutes. Microwave on DEFROST for 2 to 3 minutes, stirring once.

NUTRITION INFORMATION PER SERVING

SERVING SIZE: 1 TABLESPOON		PERCENT U.S. RDA PER SERVING	
CALORIES	80	PROTEIN	*
PROTEIN	1g	VITAMIN A	2%
CARBOHYDRATE	9g	VITAMIN C	*
FAT	4g	THIAMINE	*
CHOLESTEROL	8mg	RIBOFLAVIN	*
SODIUM	30mg	NIACIN	*
POTASSIUM	35mg	CALCIUM	*
		IRON	*

*Contains less than 2% of the U.S. RDA of this nutrient.

A super recipe for fresh fruit.

Chocolate Caramel Sauce

12 vanilla caramels, unwrapped
½ cup whipping cream
6-oz. pkg. (1 cup) semi-sweet
  chocolate chips
1 tablespoon margarine or butter
  Apples or favorite fresh fruit,
  sliced

In small saucepan over low heat, combine caramels, whipping cream, chocolate chips and margarine, stirring occasionally until smooth.

Serve warm over fruit. Store any remaining sauce in refrigerator. 1⅓ cups.

▆ MICROWAVE DIRECTIONS: In small microwave-safe bowl, combine caramels and whipping cream. Microwave on MEDIUM for 4½ to 5 minutes, stirring once. Stir until mixture is smooth. Add chocolate chips and margarine; stir until smooth.

NUTRITION INFORMATION PER SERVING

SERVING SIZE: 1 TABLESPOON		PERCENT U.S. RDA PER SERVING	
CALORIES	90	PROTEIN	*
PROTEIN	1g	VITAMIN A	2%
CARBOHYDRATE	9g	VITAMIN C	*
FAT	6g	THIAMINE	*
CHOLESTEROL	8mg	RIBOFLAVIN	*
SODIUM	20mg	NIACIN	*
POTASSIUM	40mg	CALCIUM	*
		IRON	*

*Contains less than 2% of the U.S. RDA of this nutrient.

A delicate, low-calorie cookie, crunchy with walnuts.

Chocolate Walnut Meringues

3 egg whites, room temperature
¼ teaspoon cream of tartar
  Dash salt
¾ cup sugar
3 oz. (3 squares) semi-sweet
  chocolate, melted, cooled
¼ cup ground walnuts

Heat oven to 225°F. Cover cookie sheets with parchment paper. In small bowl, beat egg whites, cream of tartar and salt until soft peaks form. Gradually add sugar; beat until stiff peaks form. Fold in melted chocolate and nuts. Drop egg white mixture by teaspoonfuls or spoon mixture into pastry bag with decorative tip and pipe 1-inch mounds onto parchment-lined cookie sheets. Bake at 225°F. for 1½ hours. Cool completely. Remove from paper. Store in covered container. 4½ dozen cookies.

NUTRITION INFORMATION PER SERVING

SERVING SIZE: 1 COOKIE		PERCENT U.S. RDA PER SERVING	
CALORIES	25	PROTEIN	*
PROTEIN	0g	VITAMIN A	*
CARBOHYDRATE	4g	VITAMIN C	*
FAT	1g	THIAMINE	*
CHOLESTEROL	0 mg	RIBOFLAVIN	*
SODIUM	5mg	NIACIN	*
POTASSIUM	10mg	CALCIUM	*
		IRON	*

*Contains less than 2% of the U.S. RDA of this nutrient.

Satin Fudge Sauce

Garnishes...
for the perfect finishing touch

What is the first thing you notice about an exquisite dessert displayed in a bakery window or served to you in an elegant restaurant? No doubt it is the presentation and garnish or decoration that makes it memorable. How wonderful to know that those eye-catching chocolate curls, leaves, pipings, shavings, filigree and other embellishments can be made in your own kitchen. We have included precise instructions for simple and ornate garnishes from several types of chocolate. Some may take a little practice and patience. But we think you will rejoice in the results of your efforts.

GRATED CHOCOLATE

To make Grated Chocolate, refrigerate bar of chocolate (any type) for 10 minutes. Using hand grater, rub bar of chocolate across grater in a back and forth motion. Clean surface frequently to prevent clogging.

WHITE CHOCOLATE PIPING

To make White Chocolate Piping, melt 4 oz. (2 cubes) almond bark or vanilla-flavored candy coating. Spoon melted chocolate into pastry bag fitted with writing tip. Pipe design directly onto dessert.

CHOCOLATE FILIGREE

To make Chocolate Filigree, melt 2 oz. semi-sweet chocolate or sweet cooking chocolate and 1½ teaspoons shortening; cool slightly. Pour chocolate mixture into small squeeze bottle or pastry bag fitted with small writing tip. Pipe a creative design directly onto dessert or onto waxed paper-covered cookie sheets. Refrigerate until chocolate is set. Transfer with spatula to dessert.

WHITE CHOCOLATE CURLS

To make White Chocolate Curls, melt about 4 oz. white chocolate. With spatula, spread in thin layers on inverted cookie sheets. Refrigerate just until firm but still pliable. Using metal spatula, scrape chocolate from pan forming curls. If chocolate is too brittle, let stand at room temperature; if too soft, chill again. Transfer curls with toothpick to dessert.

CHOCOLATE CURLS

To make Chocolate Curls, allow bar of chocolate to stand in warm place (80 to 85°F.) until slightly softened, about 10 minutes, or soften bar by wrapping in waxed paper and turning in a rotating motion in hands to warm. Using vegetable peeler, shave chocolate in long strands along smooth side of chocolate. For larger curls, draw blade over wide surface of chocolate; for small curls, pull blade along narrow side. Transfer curls with toothpick to dessert.

CHOCOLATE CUTOUTS

To make Chocolate Cutouts, melt semi-sweet or sweet cooking chocolate. Pour into waxed paper-covered cookie sheet. Spread evenly to about ⅛ to ¼-inch thickness. Refrigerate until slightly hardened, about 10 minutes. Press hors d'oeurve or small cookie cutters firmly into chocolate. Lift gently from waxed paper with spatula.

CHOCOLATE DIAMONDS

To make Chocolate Diamonds, melt semi-sweet or sweet cooking chocolate. Pour onto waxed paper-covered cookie sheet. Spread evenly to form a circle, about ⅛ to ¼-inch thick. Refrigerate until slightly hardened, about 10 minutes. Cut into diamond shapes. If chocolate becomes too soft, refrigerate a few minutes to harden. Lift gently from waxed paper with spatula.

CHOCOLATE SHAVINGS

To make Chocolate Shavings, allow wrapped large bar of chocolate (any type) to stand in warm place (80 to 85°F.) until slightly softened, about 10 minutes, or soften bar by wrapping in waxed paper and turning in rotating motion in hands to warm. Using vegetable peeler, scrape peeler against chocolate using short quick strokes.

CHOCOLATE LEAVES

To make Chocolate Leaves, melt unsweetened, semi-sweet, sweet cooking chocolate or vanilla-flavored candy coating. Brush melted chocolate evenly on underside of washed and dried non-toxic leaves (ivy, mint, lemon or rose leaves). Wipe off any chocolate that may have dripped to front side of leaf. Refrigerate leaves about 10 minutes or until chocolate is set. Apply second layer of chocolate over first layer. Refrigerate until chocolate is set. Carefully peel leaf away from chocolate. Store in refrigerator or freezer until ready to use.

Nutrition Information

Pillsbury's **NUTRI-CODED** system can help you in your daily food planning.** Below are guidelines:

SERVING SIZE: This has been determined as a typical serving for each recipe.

CALORIES: The amount of calories a person needs is determined by age, size and activity level. The recommended daily allowances generally are: 1800-2400 for women and children 4 to 10 years of age and 2400-2800 for men.

PROTEIN: The amount of protein needed daily is determined by age and size; the general U.S. RDA is 65 grams for adults and children of at least 4 years of age.

CARBOHYDRATE, FAT, CHOLESTEROL, SODIUM, AND POTASSIUM:
Recommended Dietary Allowances (RDA) for these nutrients have not been determined; however, the carbohydrate should be adequate so the body does not burn protein for energy. The American Heart Association recommendation for those who wish to restrict dietary cholesterol is for a daily intake that is less than 100 milligrams per 1000 calories and not exceeding a total of 300 milligrams.

PERCENT U.S. RDA PER SERVING: For a nutritionally balanced diet, choose recipes which will provide 100% of the U.S. Recommended Daily Allowance for each nutrient.

Pillsbury Guidelines for Calculating the Nutrition Information:

♥ When the ingredient listing gives one or more options, the first ingredient listed is the one analyzed.

♥ When a range is given for an ingredient, the larger amount is analyzed.

♥ When ingredients are listed as "if desired," these ingredients are included in the nutrition information.

♥ Serving suggestions listed in the ingredients are calculated in the nutrition information.

♥ When each bread recipe is analyzed, a serving of yeast-leavened bread is a 1-oz. slice and a quick bread serving, 1/16 of the loaf. Recipes that vary are indicated.

Symbol Meanings:

The following symbols are used in relation to the nutrition data:

    *   Less than 2% of the nutrient
   <1 Less than one gram (or milligram) of the nutrient

Any questions regarding nutrition information in this book should be addressed to:

The Pillsbury Company
Pillsbury Center—Suite 2866
Minneapolis, Minnesota 55402

**The primary source for values used in this program is the revised Agriculture Handbook No. 8 and is only as correct and complete as the information supplies.

NOTE FOR PEOPLE WITH SPECIAL DIETARY NEEDS: CONSULT YOUR PHYSICIAN REGARDING RELIANCE ON THE NUTRITION INFORMATION IN THIS BOOK.
Every effort has been made to ensure the accuracy of this information. However, The Pillsbury Company does not guarantee its suitability for specific medically imposed diets.

Index

A